高职高专"十三五"规划教材

国际商务函电

A Manual for Business English Writing

（实战篇）

主　编　舒　红　赵东明
副主编　唐苏苏　秦春淼　许定洁

微信扫码查看资源

南京大学出版社

图书在版编目(CIP)数据

国际商务函电.实战篇 / 舒红,赵东明主编. — 南京：南京大学出版社,2019.6
ISBN 978-7-305-21944-3

Ⅰ.①国… Ⅱ.①舒… ②赵… Ⅲ.①国际商务－英语－电报信函－写作－高等职业教育－教材 Ⅳ.①F740

中国版本图书馆 CIP 数据核字(2019)第 072794 号

出版发行	南京大学出版社
社　　址	南京市汉口路 22 号　　邮编　210093
出 版 人	金鑫荣
书　　名	**国际商务函电(实战篇)**
主　　编	舒　红　赵东明
责任编辑	张亚男　武　坦　　编辑热线 025 - 83592315
照　　排	南京理工大学资产经营有限公司
印　　刷	南京人民印刷厂有限责任公司
开　　本	787×1092　1/16　印张 11.5　字数 259 千
版　　次	2019 年 6 月第 1 版　2019 年 6 月第 1 次印刷
ISBN	978-7-305-21944-3
定　　价	32.00 元
网　　址	http://www.njupco.com
官方微博	http://weibo.com/njupco
微信服务号	njuyuexue
销售咨询热线	(025)83594756

* 版权所有,侵权必究
* 凡购买南大版图书,如有印装质量问题,请与所购
　图书销售部门联系调换

前　言

一、编写宗旨

笔者根据《国务院关于大力发展职业教育的决定》的文件精神，以《高等职业院校专业教学标准（试行）》为依据，本着"以职业能力为导向，以素质技能为目标"的宗旨来编写本书。

本书不求高深，遵循"应用，实用，够用"的"三用"原则，通过学习大量的一线案例，模仿职业元素极强的商务英文信函和电子邮件实战篇，以达到"读书破万卷，下笔如有神"的目的与效果。从而增强学习者的学习信心，明确学习目标，激发学习兴趣。

二、适用对象

特别适用于高职高专国际贸易、报关与国际货运、物流、商务英语、电子商务及相关专业的学生学习，也适用于本科院校的国际经济与贸易专业、国际商务专业等相关专业的学生学习。同时对工作在对外贸易前沿和相关领域的商业人士，或要从事涉外商务的人员也是一本极为珍贵的、值得借鉴的和学习参考的精品商务英文写作手册。

三、案例鲜明

本书部分英文案例，采用了主编舒红在海外国际贸易公司工作期间与欧美各国商务伙伴的原创函电，囊括和再现了各种工作过程的英文写作知识。其中的信函、传真、E-mail案例商务英文纯正、真实、浅显易懂，实用性极强。随着跨境电子商务这种新型国际贸易方式的迅速发展，与外商的英文函电的写作日益频繁。本书为此需求提供了370余篇各种案例范文，且在每小节后都配有练习题，能够及时检测学生的学习情况。

四、趣味性与知识性结合

在各小节中穿插的小知识，简短而精美，趣味性与知识性相结合，让学生在享受英语文化精品的同时，了解文化与商务背景，学习国际贸易知识，从而能更好地理解商务函电的内容。有助于拓宽学生们的知识面，为其职业发展奠定良好的基础。

五、编写团队

本书由重庆公共运输职业学院舒红、赵东明担任主编,由重庆公共运输职业学院唐苏苏、武汉工程职业技术学院秦春淼和重庆电子工程职业学院许定洁担任副主编。本书共有4章,Unit 1 由舒红编写,Unit 2 由舒红、赵东明、秦春淼、许定洁编写,Unit 3 由赵东明编写,Unit 4 由唐苏苏编写。舒红负责全书统稿工作。同时由衷感谢美国旧金山 Golden Bay Trading Company(金海湾国际贸易有限公司)CEO,副总裁 Mr. Eddie Dominik 对本书英文部分的校正。

最后,恳请广大读者对书中存在的疏漏之处批评指正,并提出宝贵的建议。

编　者

2019 年 5 月

CONTENTS

Unit 1　Format of Business English Letters ········· (1)

  1　Layout of Business Letter-writing ········· (1)
  2　Format of Business Letter-writing ········· (5)
  3　Addressing Envelopes ········· (7)
  4　Layout of Business E-mail ········· (8)

Unit 2　Body of Business English Letters ········· (13)

  1　The International Fair ········· (13)
  2　Appreciation ········· (25)
  3　Invitation ········· (35)
  4　Reservation ········· (45)
  5　Notification ········· (52)
  6　Recommendation ········· (62)
  7　Sales Promotion ········· (68)
  8　Placing Orders ········· (76)
  9　Payment ········· (85)
  10　A Credit Reference ········· (96)
  11　Job Search ········· (99)
  12　Product Consultation ········· (106)
  13　Claims and Settlement ········· (117)
  14　Quotation ········· (127)

1

15　Business Negotiation ……………………………………………… (129)
　　16　Apology …………………………………………………………… (135)
　　17　Visiting …………………………………………………………… (137)
　　18　Condolences ……………………………………………………… (140)

Unit 3　Common Business E-mail Collection ……………………… (143)

　　1　Landing a Dream Job …………………………………………… (143)
　　2　My Visit to San Francisco ……………………………………… (144)
　　3　Response for Visit to San Francisco …………………………… (144)
　　4　Change of My E-mail Address ………………………………… (145)
　　5　Finding a Host Family …………………………………………… (145)
　　6　Mail-order Catalog ……………………………………………… (146)
　　7　My Order for the Everflo Baby Carriage ……………………… (146)
　　8　Reply on Your Order of Baby Carriage ……………………… (147)
　　9　Job Application with Resume …………………………………… (147)
　　10　Inviting to Job Interview ……………………………………… (148)
　　11　Confirm an Appointment ……………………………………… (149)
　　12　Requesting a Meeting ………………………………………… (149)
　　13　Thanks for a Warm Reception ………………………………… (150)
　　14　Team Meeting on Project Z …………………………………… (150)
　　15　Clarification of Assigned Task ………………………………… (151)
　　16　Request for Vacation …………………………………………… (151)
　　17　I will be on Vacation …………………………………………… (152)
　　18　Interested in Your Services …………………………………… (152)
　　19　Appreciate Your Referral ……………………………………… (153)
　　20　Visit Our New Website ………………………………………… (153)

Unit 4　Useful Sentence for Business E-mail …………………… (156)

　　1　Usual Greetings …………………………………………………… (156)
　　2　Greetings of Special Day ………………………………………… (157)
　　3　Grateful Expression ……………………………………………… (157)
　　4　Apologizing ………………………………………………………… (158)
　　5　Thanks for Replying ……………………………………………… (158)
　　6　Recent Situation …………………………………………………… (159)

CONTENTS

    7   The Reception Invitation ··· (159)

    8   To Inform and Inquire ··· (159)

    9   Confirming Information ··· (160)

    10   Requesting Help ·· (160)

    11   Shopping ·· (160)

    12   Expressing Your Opinion ··· (161)

    13   Complain ··· (162)

    14   Appointments and Commitments ·· (162)

    15   The Complementary Close ·· (162)

    16   Greetings of Closing ·· (163)

Appendix ·· (164)

    1   Common Abbreviations ·· (164)

    2   Department and Job Title of Companies ·· (166)

    3   World's Major Ports ·· (167)

References ··· (172)

目 录

Unit 1　商务英文函电的格式 ……………………………………………………（1）

　　1　商务信函布局 ……………………………………………………………（1）
　　2　商务信函版式 ……………………………………………………………（5）
　　3　信　封 ……………………………………………………………………（7）
　　4　电子邮件布局 ……………………………………………………………（8）

Unit 2　商务英文函电正文内容 …………………………………………………（13）

　　1　参加世界展销会 …………………………………………………………（13）
　　2　感谢函电 …………………………………………………………………（25）
　　3　邀请函 ……………………………………………………………………（35）
　　4　预约函 ……………………………………………………………………（45）
　　5　通　知 ……………………………………………………………………（52）
　　6　介绍推荐函 ………………………………………………………………（62）
　　7　推　销 ……………………………………………………………………（68）
　　8　下订单 ……………………………………………………………………（76）
　　9　付　款 ……………………………………………………………………（85）
　　10　信用查询 …………………………………………………………………（96）
　　11　求　职 ……………………………………………………………………（99）
　　12　咨　询 ……………………………………………………………………（106）
　　13　争议与处理 ………………………………………………………………（117）
　　14　预　算 ……………………………………………………………………（127）
　　15　交易蹉商 …………………………………………………………………（129）
　　16　道　歉 ……………………………………………………………………（135）
　　17　探　望 ……………………………………………………………………（137）
　　18　慰　问 ……………………………………………………………………（140）

Unit 3　常用商务 E-mail 案例集 ·················· (143)

 1 找到理想的工作 ·················· (143)
 2 访问旧金山 ·················· (144)
 3 回复来访旧金山 ·················· (144)
 4 邮箱地址变更 ·················· (145)
 5 寻找寄宿家庭 ·················· (145)
 6 邮购的商品目录 ·················· (146)
 7 订购 Everflo 牌婴儿手推车 ·················· (146)
 8 回复订购婴儿手推车 ·················· (147)
 9 附有简历的工作申请 ·················· (147)
 10 工作面试的通知 ·················· (148)
 11 确认预约 ·················· (149)
 12 请求面谈 ·················· (149)
 13 感谢热情接待 ·················· (150)
 14 有关项目 Z 的团队会议 ·················· (150)
 15 明确工作责任 ·················· (151)
 16 请求休假 ·················· (151)
 17 休假通知 ·················· (152)
 18 对公司的服务感兴趣 ·················· (152)
 19 感谢对本公司的介绍 ·················· (153)
 20 本公司的网页已刷新 ·················· (153)

Unit 4　常用 E-mail 经典句案例集 ·················· (156)

 1 一般的问候 ·················· (156)
 2 特别日子的问候 ·················· (157)
 3 谢礼表达 ·················· (157)
 4 赔礼道歉 ·················· (158)
 5 对回信的感谢 ·················· (158)
 6 传达近况 ·················· (159)
 7 招待邀请 ·················· (159)
 8 通知和询问 ·················· (159)
 9 确认信息 ·················· (160)
 10 请求帮助 ·················· (160)
 11 购　物 ·················· (160)
 12 阐明意见 ·················· (161)

13　表达不满 …………………………………………………… (162)
 14　预约及承诺 ………………………………………………… (162)
 15　正文结束语 ………………………………………………… (162)
 16　结束问候语 ………………………………………………… (163)

附　录 ……………………………………………………………… (164)

 1　函电常用缩写语 …………………………………………… (164)
 2　公司常见部门及职务名称 ………………………………… (166)
 3　世界主要港口 ……………………………………………… (167)

参考文献 …………………………………………………………… (172)

Unit 1

Format of Business English Letters
商务英文函电的格式

> **Aims to Obtain**
> **After the completion of the whole course, students are supposed to:**
> - comprehend and master the basic writing rules and skills for various types of business correspondence;
> - be familiar with the layout and format of Business Letter-Writing;
> - know how to write envelope of business letters;
> - be familiar with the layout of Business E-mail.

1 Layout of Business Letter-writing
商务信函布局

1-1 信头 Letter Head

一般说来,信头指写信人的公司,包括公司名称、地址、电话、传真、邮箱、Web 等信息,在信的最上方比较醒目地展示出来。有的公司把印有公司 Logo 和以上信息的内容提前打印在信纸的上方。

1-2 日期 Date

这个是指写信的日期(Writing Date),一般在右上方信头下的位置,有美国式和英国式两种写法:

美国式为 June 3,2019　　　　　　英国式为 3rd June,2019

1

1-3　封内地址 Inside Address

封内地址是指收信人公司，一般在函电的左上方。内容包含收信人公司的名字，地址，电话，传真，邮箱，邮政编码等信息。

1-4　经办人 Attention Line

当不知道写信给某特定人的名字时，可以用组织名、部门名或职务名代替。例如，Department of Journalism，Sales manager 等。

1-5　称呼 Salutation

在商务函电中，通常在对方人名前加上"Dear"一词，不仅仅是亲近的含义也表达对收信人的敬意和礼貌。不知道对方的名字时，可用 Dear Sales Manager，Dear Customer，如果是复数直接加 s，Dear Customers，Dear Sirs or Madams。常用的还有 Ladies and Gentlemen。在称呼后多用冒号（：），表明更正式，更专业。

例如，对方名字为男性 John Smith，可称呼为 Dear Mr. Smith，or Dear John（比较熟悉的情况）。

1-6　事由 Subject /Re：＝Regarding

事由就是函电内容的关键词，让对方一目了然想表达的主要内容和写信目的。按英式写法，一般要在事由或信件名前加 Re：(Re 来自拉丁语，是关于的意思)。例如，Re：Discount of Products（有关产品折扣的事宜）。

1-7　正文 Body

正文是函电中最重要的部分，陈述写信人的目的，必须了解写信的技巧和一些原则。正文内容要以 5C 为原则，即 Correctness（正确），Conciseness（简洁），Clearness（清晰），Consideration（尊重对方文化），Courtesy（有礼貌），才能写出高效的函电。在正文开始前，一般要有一个承上启下的寒暄语，如 Thank you for your usual support 等；正文结束后也有一个惯用结束语，如 Your prompt reply would be very much appreciated 等。

1-8　结尾敬语 Complimentary Close

在最后的一般性礼貌用语，相当于中文的"祝身体健康，万事如意"之类的功能。一般正式的用 Sincerely，Very truly yours，Yours faithfully，Yours truly，Yours sincerely 等。比较随意的有 Thanks and best regards. Best Wishes. Yours.等。

1-9　签名 Signature

在欧美等西方国家,写信人没有用红色印章盖章的习惯,而是用别人难以模仿、自己独特的签字来署名。通常也有在署名下再正式地打一遍名字的习惯,为了让对方清楚地确认名字的拼写字母。例如:

International Industry Inc.

Jack Smith

Jack Smith, Sales Manager

1-10　参考号 Ref. No. = Reference No.

根据函电中交付的部门或商品类别的不同,为函电编写一个号码,以便日后能从大量的函电中迅速找到相对应的函电。这个在业务繁忙的外贸公司中经常被使用。

1-11　附件 Encl, = Enclosure

在写信的同时,还在信封里附有商品目录或价格表等资料时就要指明 Encl, catalog or price-list. 除了邮寄外,电子邮件的附件也可用 Encl,表示。

1-12　抄送 Carbon Copy(CC.)

写信人在给对方写信时,同时又抄送一份给第三者,就用 CC.＋第三者名或第三者的电子邮件名。对方知道写信人是给第三者抄送了一份。

(1-10～1-12)写信人可根据情况自行判断是否需要添加。

1-13　密送 Blind Carbon Copy(BCC.)

写信人在给对方写信时,同时又秘密发送一份给第三者,就用 BCC.＋第三者名或第三者的电子邮件名。要注意,对方不知道写信人给第三者抄送了一份,因此称为密送。选用 CC 还是 BCC 要根据写信人的商业状况来决定。

1-14　追加 Postscript(PS)

在正文中忘记写的内容,可在此追加,同时也起到强调的作用。

例如,PS: Price are currently rising. We urge you to order promptly.（价格在上涨,请尽快下订单。）

实用案例

Tokyo Shoes Import & Export Co., Ltd 【信头（写信人）】

5-3-18, Ikebukuro

Toshima-ku, 171-0014, Tokyo, Japan.

Tel: 81-3-54597378　Fax: 81-3-54597379

www.tkshoes.com.net

Our reference No.2687 【参考号】

March 5, 2019 【写信日期】

Broncolor Fashion Co., Ltd 【封内地址（收信人）】

Hyopara Jabetu 6, P.O. Box 1

00581　London, England

Attention: Sales director 【经办人】

Re: introduction of company 【事由】

Dear Sir: 【称呼】

We owe your name and address to the Commercial Counselor's Office of the Finnish Embassy in Tokyo who have informed us that you are in the market for Textiles. 【正文】

We avail ourselves of this opportunity to approach you for the establishment of trade relations with you.

In our trade with merchants of various countries, we always adhere to the principle of equality and mutual benefit. We look forward to receiving your inquiries soon.

Yours faithfully 【结尾敬语】

Tokyo Textile Import and Export Trading Co., Ltd

Tanaka Michiko 【签名】　Tanaka Michiko

Encl: catalog 【附件】

CC: John Smith 【抄送】

BCC: Jack Bron 【密送】

PS: 【追加】 It is our hope to trade with you.

2 Format of Business Letter-writing
商务信函版式

2-1 平头式 Block Format

The block format is the simplest format; all of the writing is flush against the left margin.

China National Light Industrial Products
Import & Export Corporation
82 Tian'anmen Street, Beijing, China
Tel:86 - 10 - 87336868   Fax:86 - 10 - 87336869

March 5, 2019
Nippon international trading co.Ltd
3 Nihonbashi, honcho 5 chome
Tokyo, Japan

Gentleman:
Thank you for your letter of January 10 and shall be glad to enter into business relations with your firm.
We are a state-operated corporation, handling both the import and export of Light Industrial Products. In order to acquaint you with our business lines, we enclose herewith a copy of our catalog covering the main items that are available at present.
Should any of the items be of interest to you, please let us know, we shall be glad to give you our lowest quotations upon receipt of your detailed requirements.
We are looking forward to hearing from you soon.
Very Truly Yours

China National Light Industrial Products
Import & Export Corporation
Liu Xiaoliang   president

2-2 缩头式 The Indented Format

Also the first line of each paragraph is indented.

China National Light Industrial Products

Import & Export Corporation

82 Tian'anmen Street, Beijing, China

Tel:86 - 10 - 87336868 Fax:86 - 10 - 87336869

March 27, 2019

Nippon international trading co.Ltd

3 Nihonbashi, honcho 5 chome

Tokyo, Japan

Gentleman:

  Thank you for your letter of January 10 and shall be glad to enter into business relations with your firm.

  We are a state-operated corporation, handling both the import and export of Light Industrial Products. In order to acquaint you with our business lines, we enclose herewith a copy of our catalog covering the main items that are available at present.

  Should any of the items be of interest to you, please let us know, we shall be glad to give you our lowest quotations upon receipt of your detailed requirements.

  We are looking forward to hearing from you soon.

Very Truly Yours

China National Light Industrial Products

Import & Export Corporation

Liu Xiaoliang sales manager

2-3 混合式 The Semi-block Format

Date, the closing, signature, are all indented to the right half of the page.

China National Light Industrial Products

Import & Export Corporation

82 Tian'anmen Street, Beijing, China

Tel:86 - 10 - 87336868 Fax:86 - 10 - 87336869

March 5, 2019

Nippon international trading co.Ltd

3 Nihonbashi, honcho 5 chome

Tokyo, Japan

Gentleman：

Thank you for your letter of January 10 and shall be glad to enter into business relations with your firm.

We are a state-operated corporation, handling both the import and export of Light Industrial Products. In order to acquaint you with our business lines, we enclose herewith a copy of our catalog covering the main items that are available at present.

Should any of the items be of interest to you, please let us know, we shall be glad to give you our lowest quotations upon receipt of your detailed requirements.

We are looking forward to hearing from you soon.

Very Truly Yours

China National Light Industrial Products

Import&Export Corporation

Liu Xiaoliang president

3 Addressing Envelopes
   信　封

信封的写法如下所示：

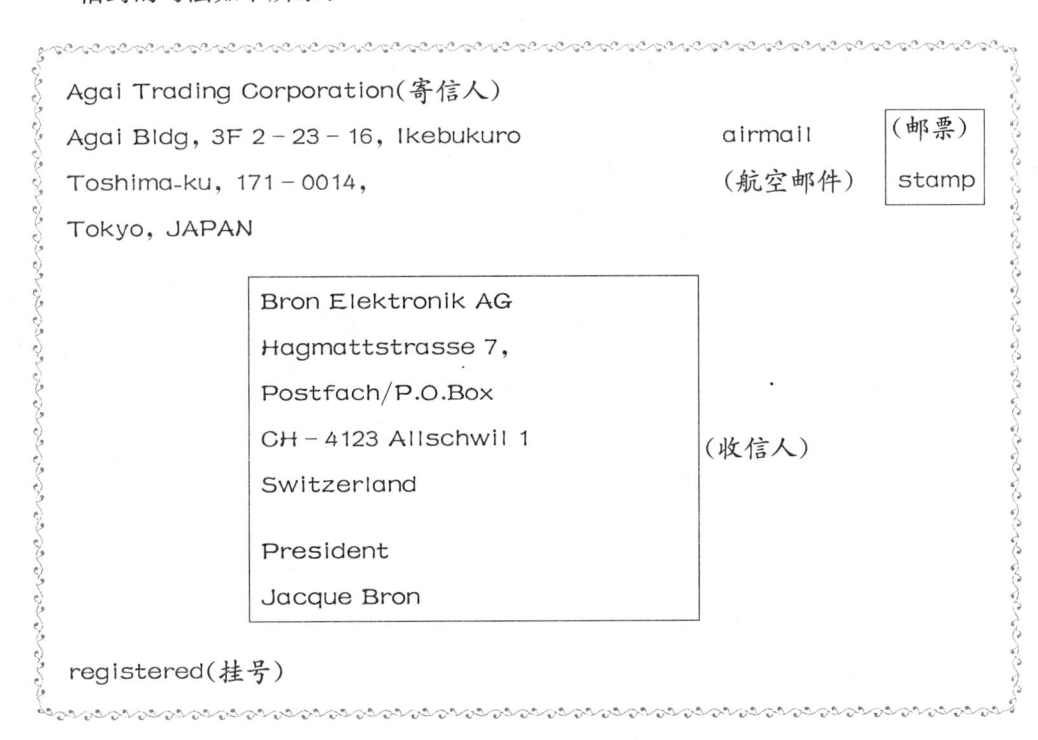

```
Agai Trading Corporation(寄信人)
Agai Bldg, 3F 2-23-16, Ikebukuro        airmail        (邮票)
Toshima-ku, 171-0014,                  (航空邮件)      stamp
Tokyo, JAPAN

            Bron Elektronik AG
            Hagmattstrasse 7,
            Postfach/P.O.Box
            CH-4123 Allschwil 1         (收信人)
            Switzerland

            President
            Jacque Bron

registered(挂号)
```

4　Layout of Business E-mail
电子邮件布局

电子邮件包含以下内容：

发件人 From；

收件人 To；

日期 Date

事由/件名 Subject

抄送 Carbon Copy(CC)

密送 Blind Carbon Copy(BCC)

称呼 Salutation

正文 Body

结尾敬语 Complimentary Close

签名 Signature

附件 Enclosure / Attachment

电子邮件和信函的框架结构基本相同。不同点在于"From:发件人"这栏写发件人电子邮箱地址，"To:收件人"这栏写收件人电子邮箱地址。

4-1　外发邮件的框架

外发邮件框架如图1-1所示。

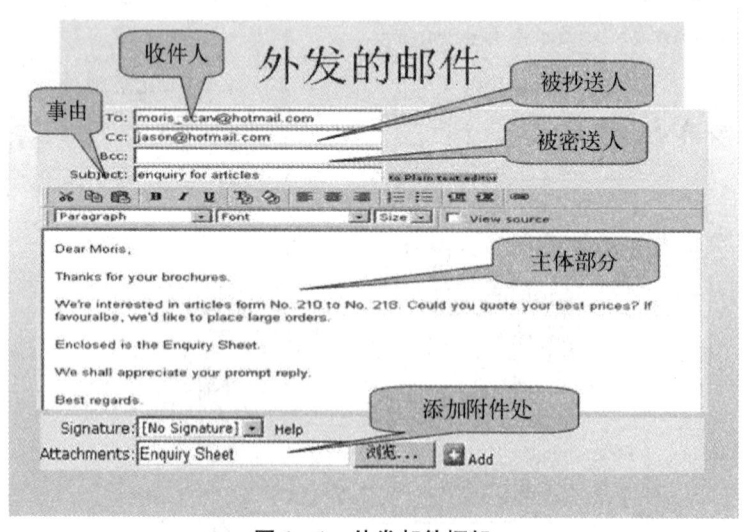

图1-1　外发邮件框架

实用案例

To: Farnik Claudia

Sent: Monday, August 23, 2019 5:30 PM

Subject: travel spot

BCC: Claude Bron

Dear Miss Sylvia Bader and Miss Claudia,

We are now considering to have a short tour about Sep. 25 2019 in Switzerland before we go to Germany.

We heard that there are many natural marvelous scenery in your country, and we really would like to enjoy them with such a valuable opportunity.

Could you recommend some beautiful place for us to visit? Your kind advice would be very much appreciated.

Thanks & best regards,

Shu Hong

Agai Trading Corporation

Agai Bldg, 3F 2-23-16, Ikebukuro

Toshima-ku, 171-0014, Tokyo, JAPAN

TEL: +81-3-5954-7577   FAX: +81-3-5954-7578

E-mail: info@agai-jp.com

http://www.agai-jp.com

Notes:

另外,在中国还有以下3种被广泛应用的联系方式

Wechat(微信号)366889321

QQ: 1572348

mobile phone: 1896889321

4-2 接收邮件的框架

接收邮件框架如图1-2所示。

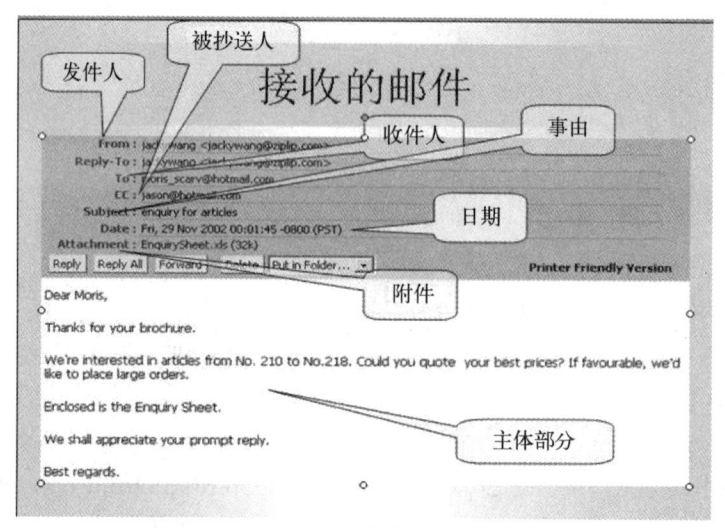

图 1-2　接收邮件框架

实用案例

From: Farnik Claudia

To: "Agai Trading Corporation"

Sent date: Tuesday, August 24, 2019 9:34 PM

Subject: AW: travel spot

CC: Ishiki

Attachment: travel map

Dear Shu,

I am looking very much forward to meeting you either in Switzerland or in Cologne at Photokina.

Sylvia Bader has sent you an E-mail with all the nice spots which are worthy to be visited.

Is there anything planned for sure? Will you visit Bron Elektronik? Hopefully the weather will show its sunny face. Please let us know the details of your trip.

Best regards,
Claudia Farnik

Bron Elektronik AG

Communications

Hagmattstrasse 7

CH – 4123 Allschwil

Switzerland

Phone　　+41 61 485 85 83

Fax　　　+41 61 485 85 00

www.bron.ch

Exercise

Elanbach

Llangoed Hall, Llyswen

Brecon, Powys, LD3 0YP, UK

+44 (0)1874 754 631 (T)

+44 (0)1874 754 588 (F)

www.elanbach.com

December 18, 2019

Guangzhou Textile Import & Export Co.Ltd

18 – 3 Fengjiang Road, Guangzhou City,

Guangdong, 527500, China

Attention: Business Manager

Re: bags

Dear Sir,

　　Thank you for your usual support.

　　I have read your E-mail about the bags and I am not sure what we can do to make the bags better. The sewing is done in a large factory at low cost and high speed. Using this route, we will never be able to make the bags 100% perfect at the cost we supply them to you. They are a mass produced bag as I have mentioned in previous emails. I may have found another bag maker this morning but I will have to get some samples made to see if their quality is any better.

　　I'm sorry it has taken me so long to get back to you.

Best regards,

Simon Maynard

For and on Behalf of Elanbach

Encl. latest price list

CC: Parak Maynard

1. Read the aboved letter, fill in the blanks with the correct information (English).

   Name of Sender _____

   Fax number of Sender _____

   Writing Date _____

   Attention _____

   Subject Line _____

   Name of Receiver _____

   Address of Receiver _____

   Complimentary Close _____

   Signature _____

   Enclosure/Attachment _____

   CC to _____

2. According to the above mentioned letter, write an envelope (send by airmail).

Unit 2

Body of Business English Letters
商务英文函电正文内容

▶ 1　The International Fair
　　　参加世界展销会

Aims to Obtain

Upon completion of the unit, you should:
- know how to write fax, invitation, visa application ticket and hotel booking, etc. before fair;
- know how to write letters to establish business relations;
- be able to negotiate with your foreign clients.

1-1　发送邀请函的传真

实用案例

```
              Bron Elektronik AG  发件人
      Hagmattstrasse 7    Telefon   +41 61-485 85 85
      Postfach/P.O.Box    Fax       +41 61-485 85 00
      CH-4123 Allschwil 1  E-Mail   info@bron.ch
          Schweiz/Switzerland      www.bron.ch

  Telefax 传真
```

13

To: GERMAN EMBASSY, Tokyo　　　收件人

Date: 9 September 2018

Page: 1 of 3

Re: INVITATION for Miss SHU HONG　　(regarding) 事由

Dear Madam or Sir,

　　Please find attached our invitation letter for Miss SHU HONG of AGAI TRADING CORP. As well as a copy of her entry ticket to the Photokina exhibition, referring to the visa application made by Miss Shu Hong.

　　　　　　　　　　　　　　　　　　　　　　　Best regards

BRON ELEKTRONIK AG

S. Bader　　发件人签名

Sylvia Bader

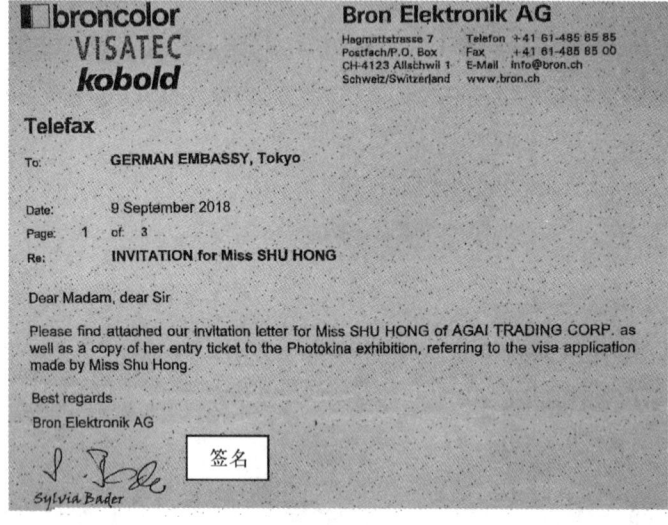

展销会门票

Words and Expressions

1. find attached 查收附件
2. entry ticket to the exhibition 展销会门票

3. refer to 关于
4. the Photokina exhibition 影像博览会
5. visa application 签证申请

小知识　　　　　　　　　**The Photokina Exhibition**

　　两年一届的世界影像博览会(photokina)，在德国著名的会展城科隆举行，是摄影与成像工业领域领先的展览会，是世界上唯一为大众消费者和专业人士提供所有成像介质、成像技术与成像市场综合性展示的展览会。因此，世界影像展览会在成像领域具有独特的竞争优势，使其成为所有影像用户提供综合性解决方案的展示平台。世界影像博览会不仅为照相与成像产业部门提供新的销售动力，而且是集中展示面向未来的各种技术和产品的趋势论坛。

　　在新的"影像无限"的主题下，2016科隆世界影像博览会(photokina)为参展商、观众和媒体带来了许多启迪。确定新的目标群体是迈向未来世界领先照片、视频、成像博览会的重要第一步。当前，新的主题不断涌现，这将是一个崭新的阶段，一个全新的时代。

德国科隆展览中心

Bron Elektronik AG(瑞士布朗摄影器材公司)展台(中间站立者为主编舒红，2004年)

1-2 参展邀请函

Ⅰ.海外参展

INVITATION

We, Bron Elektronik AG, manufacturers of studio lighting equipment in Allschwil, Switzerland, offcially invite our distributor in Tokyo Agai Trading Corporation, including staff Ms. Shu Hong, to visit our factory and see the Photokina fair 2018 in the period of 26 September to 29 September 2018.

Ⅱ.国内参展

We are China Business Guide of MOFCOM (Ministry of Commerce) Public Information Service, a non-profit governmental organization like JETRO in Japan, TDC in Hong Kong China and KOTRA in the Republic of Korea.

We are dedicated to assisting China small and medium-sized businesses on a free-of-charge basis to extend the international market and promote the mutual trade relations with the corporations and trade organizations worldwide.

We are here inviting you, on behalf of the organizer to attend the 25th China Kunming Export Commodities Fair (Kunming Fair) to be held at Kunming International Trade Center on 12th to 18th June, 2020.

For more details of the fair, please refer to the website http://www.kmfair.org.

Words and Expressions

1. MOFCOM (Ministry of Commerce) 商务部
2. distributor 经销商；代理
3. manufacturer 制造商
4. non-profit governmental organization 非营利性政府组织
5. JETRO 日本贸易振兴机构
6. TDC 香港贸易发展局
7. KOTRA 大韩贸易投资振兴公社
8. be dedicated to doing 专心致志于……
9. extend the international market 扩大国际市场
10. the mutual trade relations 双边贸易关系
11. on behalf of 代表……

1-3 请求大使馆发行签证

Ⅰ. 申根签证

Embassy of Germany,

Enclosed is a letter in regard to the statement of employee Shu Hong's business trip to Germany. Kindly issue the necessary travel documents to Ms Shu Hong.

Shu Hong joined Agai Trading Corporation on March 6, 2016. She is charge of communicating daily affairs of company to overseas, such as German, Switzerland, Hong Kong, China, etc. Her income is JPY 180,000 each month.

The purpose of this business trip is to see photokina 2018, one of the biggest photographic exhibitions in the world, which is taken place in Cologne, Germany every two years.

The stay period is from Sep. 26 to Sep. 29, 2018 (enter into Frankfruit, in the morning on Sep. 26 and go out of Germany in the morning on Sep. 29). The round trip air fare is JPY 81,500. Company will take all charge of travel expenses including air fare.

Words and Expressions

1. Embassy 大使馆
2. issue 发行
3. business trip 出差
4. income 收入
5. be charge of 负责
6. the round trip air fare 往返机票费

小知识　　　　Schengen Visa(申根签证)

申根签证(Schengen Visa)是指根据欧洲申根协议而签发的签证。这项协议由于在卢森堡的申根签署而得名。协议规定任何一个申根成员国签发的签证,在所有其他成员国也被视作有效,而无须另外申请签证。实施这项协议的国家便是通常所说的"申根国家"。

截至2013年年底,申根的成员国增加到奥地利、比利时、丹麦、芬兰、法国、德国、冰岛、意大利、希腊、卢森堡、荷兰、挪威、葡萄牙、西班牙、瑞典、瑞士等26个国家。假如你申请到了意大利的签证,其他所有申根国家你都可以自由进出。

Ⅱ. 美国签证

AGAI TRADING CORPORATION

1F Agai building, 2-23-16, lkebukuro, Toshima-ku, Tokyo, 171-0014 JAPAN
TEL:+81-3-5954-7577   FAX:+81-3-5954-7578   E-mail:info@agai-jp.com

Attn: Embassy of the United States, Japan

Date: 1 November 2018

Number of page(s): 1

Re: issuing tourism visa for Shu Hong

Dear Madam or sir,

We, Agai Trading Corporation, an import and export of studio lighting equipment for professional photographer, planned a staff tour for mutual understanding and friendship among all staffs including staff Ms. Shu Hong at Hawaii in the definite temporary period of 13 December to 17 December, 2018. We are planning to hold a friendship party with our all staffs to appreciate everyone's hard work during 2018 in Hawaii.

We hereby guarantee that Ms.Shu Hong who has been working at Agai Trading Corporation over four and half years and had a stable monthly salary 250,000 Japanese yen must return back to Tokyo, Japan upon the conclusion of visit according to the schedule attached. Company will cover all expenses for her trip including flight, accommodation fee, etc.

Kindly issue the necessary visa to Ms Shu Hong.

Sincerely
Agai Trading Corporation
Managing Director
Satoko Ono

Words and Expressions

1. tourism visa 旅行签证
2. mutual 双边的
3. temporary 暂时的
4. hereby 在此(正式的)
5. guarantee 保证
6. a stable monthly salary 稳定的月收入
7. schedule 日程安排表
8. accommodation fee 住宿费

1-4 参展前的观光咨询

We are considering to have a tour about Sep. 25 in Switzerland before we go to Germany.

We heard that there are many natural marvelous scenery in your country, and we really would like to enjoy them with such a valuable opportunity.

Could you recommend some beautiful place for us to visit? Your kind advice would be very much appreciated.

Words and Expressions

1. marvelous 精彩的
2. a valuable opportunity 有价值的机会
3. recommend 推荐
4. appreciate 感激

1-5 回复和推荐观光景点

Already now WELCOME TO SWITZERLAND!

There are many beautiful regions to be visited in Switzerland. Specially nice place to see is：

——the city of Lucerne on the lake of Lucerne with the mountains Pilatus and Rigi (trains and cable cars go up to the peak). For further details please see www.lucerne.org.

Time needed to go from Basel to Lucerne：approx. one hour by train or car.

I hope this is the type of places you are looking for. If I can be of further assistance, just let me know.

Words and Expressions

1. region 地区
2. the lake of Lucerne 卢塞恩湖(瑞士)
3. further assistance 进一步的支持
4. peak 顶点；山峰；最高点
5. approx(approximate) 大约

小知识   Lucerne

Lucerne 中文译名"卢塞恩",又译"琉森",是琉森州的首府,位于瑞士中部,罗伊斯河出口与四州湖的汇合处,面积24.2平方千米,人口7.8万(2017年),属于瑞士德语区，德语名为 Luzern。

位于瑞士 Pilatus 和 Rigi 山下的卢塞恩湖的湖光山色举世闻名，号称是瑞士最美丽、最理想的旅游城市，也是最受瑞士人喜爱的瑞士度假地。琉森是座历史文化名城，艺术家们在此得到了不尽的灵感。历史上，很多著名作家在此居住和写作。

1-6 订机票

I would like to buy a round trip to London, and I am leaving next Tuesday, Jan. 15, 2018. My name is Jack Liu. My ID is 510202198511035623. I need a seat of Economy, flight CA 941, 9:30 am departure. Thank you.

Words and Expressions

1. a round trip 往返
2. Economy 经济舱
3. departure 出发

1-7 订酒店

I would like to reserve a double room with Ocean view. I will be accompanied by my wife. My name is Helen Xie, the cell phone is 13992398060. Please make a reservation for one week from November 1st to the 7th 2018. Thank you.

Words and Expressions

1. a double room 双人间
2. ocean view 海景
3. accompany 陪伴
4. make a reservation 预订

1-8 接机请求

This is to confirm that Mr. Ron Young will arrive at London International Airport at 10:30 p.m. October 25, 2019 on JAL Flight♯1330.

Will you kindly meet him at the airport upon arrival? Mr. Ron Young will be carrying a brown umbrella. Your assistance will be very much appreciated.

Words and Expressions

1. confirm 确认
2. umbrella 伞
3. assistance 支持

1-9 建立业务关系

We saw your fat-reducing tea at the International Exhibition of National Health Products held in Italy during October, and are keenly interested in this product.

With a view to building trade relations with you, we are writing to you and hope to receive your catalogues and price-lists for reference.

As one of the leading American importers of health products, we are experiencing in pushing sales of the products and have good connections with wholesalers and retailers in the country. If your prices are in line, we trust important business can materialize.

We look forward to your early reply.

Words and Expressions

1. fat-reducing tea 减肥茶
2. keenly 敏锐地；强烈地
3. catalogue 商品目录
4. wholesalers 批发商
5. retailers 零售商
6. materialize 实现

1-10 交易磋商

Ⅰ.询盘

We have read your advertisement in Economic Reporter and we are glad to know that you are one of the leading exporters of silks in China. We are interested in the products and would like to be informed of details of your various types, including sizes, colors and prices.

We are large dealers in silk garments, having over 15 years' experience in this particular line of business. Silk blouse of good quality and moderate prices command a good sale in our market.

When replying, please state terms of payment and discounts you would allow on purchases of quantities of over 100 dozen of individual items.

We look forward to your early reply.

Words and Expressions

1. advertisement 广告
2. blouse 女士衬衣
3. moderate 合理的
4. terms of payment 支付条款
5. individual 各自的

Ⅱ. 发盘

We warmly welcome your enquiry of April 4 and thank you for your interest in our products. We are enclosing samples and price list of garments giving the details you asked for. We feel confident that you will find the goods both excellent in quality and reasonable in price.

Words and Expressions

1. enquiry 询问
2. confident 自信
3. reasonable 合理的

小知识　　　　国际贸易的订单取决于发盘的时间和速度

根据外贸经验,及时快速的发盘速度是促成国际贸易订单的重要因素之一。在上班办公时间收到外商邮件就立刻回复,这是比较正确的做法。因为时差的问题,有时发来邮件时国内可能是半夜或者凌晨,做不到立刻回复邮件。但是有些极其重要的商务邮件即使是在半夜或者凌晨也要回复。要吃得苦才行,订单不是那么容易就能接到的。做国际贸易的业务员要能吃苦耐劳说的就是这个,而不是要去下苦力搬运货物。

所以,商务邮件的发送与回复时间和速度是非常重要的!与海外客户紧密的、恰到好处的邮件联系不仅能使公司的订单大增,还能加强海外客户对我们的信任。

Ⅲ. 还盘

We acknowledge with thanks receipt of your offer of May 8 for the subject goods. In reply, we regret to say that we can't accept it. Your prices are rather on the high side and out of line with the world market. Information indicates that some parcels of Indian make have been sold at a much lower level.

Words and Expressions

1. acknowledge 承认,告知,感谢
2. the subject goods 标题项下的商品
3. indicate 指示
4. out of line 出格,不得体,不合理

小知识　　　　　　　　还盘的技巧

国际贸易中的还盘,通俗的说就是讨价还价.国内贸易需要讨价还价,国际贸易仍然要进行讨价还价。无论海外卖方出的什么价格,即使是能接受的心理价位,都要说太贵了,能否便宜一点,以争取最好的进口价格。在用英文说价格便宜一点时,最好不用 cheap 一词。因为 cheap 给外商的感觉,就是那种品质较差的商品。如果要让他们价格便宜一点,最好说 Could you quote us lower price/competitive price/best price? 这3种说法中的任何一种。

Ⅳ. 接受

We accept your offer of 10th Sep. 2019. The offer is "red star" gloves 2 000 dozen HK $ 3.50 per dozen CIF London shipment during July payment in sight irrevocable L/C. We will place an order for 2 000 dozen gloves. Please delivery us ASAP.

Words and Expressions

1. sight irrevocable L/C 即期不可撤销信用证
2. place an order 下订单
3. dozen 一打(12 个)
4. delivery 发送
5. ASAP (As Soon As Possible) 尽快

Exercise

Ⅰ. Fill in the blanks with the following words.

cover	confirm	reference	hold	early	assistance
issue	regret	valuable	command		

1. Kindly _____ the necessary travel documents to Ms Wang.
2. Silk blouse of good quality and moderate prices _____ a good sale in our market.
3. This is to _____ that Mr. Ron Young will arrive at London International Airport.
4. We really would like to enjoy them with such a _____ opportunity.
5. Your _____ will be very much appreciated.
6. In reply, we _____ to say that we can't accept it.
7. We are writing to you and hope to receive your catalogues and price-lists for _____ .
8. We look forward to your _____ reply.
9. We are planning to _____ a friendship party with our all staffs to appreciate everyone's hard work during 2005 in Hawaii.
10. Company will _____ all expenses for her trip.

Ⅱ. Translate the following words and phrases.

Section A: Translate into English.

1. 下订单
2. 往返票
3. 签证
4. 国际展览会
5. 预定双人间

Section B: Translate into Chinese.

1. mutual understanding
2. promote the mutual trade relations
3. guarantee
4. extend the international market
5. accommodation fee

Ⅲ. Writing in English.

请给你的贸易伙伴写一封参加第二届中国国际进口博览会的邀请函。

2 Appreciation
感谢函电

> **Aims to Obtain**
>
> **Upon completion of the unit, you should:**
> - know how to write letters to appreciate your clients, friends, etc.;
> - know how to reply sorts of invitaions;
> - be able to extend congratulations with your foreign clients.

2-1 出差归来的感谢函电(1)

Now that I have returned from my trip, I wish to thank you for all the nice things you did for me during my stay in London. Your hospitality made my trip both enjoyable and rewarding. I was particularly impressed by the latest model of equipment installed in your laboratory.

Please convey my appreciation and greetings to Mrs. Peter song. I do hope that, in the near future, I will be able to reciprocate your kindness. Thank you again.

Words and Expressions

1. hospitality 殷勤好客；招待
2. rewarding 有报酬的
3. particularly 特别；尤其
4. the latest model of equipment 最新的设备模型
5. install 安装；安顿
6. laboratory 实验室
7. convey my appreciation 表达我的感激之情
8. reciprocate 互换；回报

2-2 出差归来的感谢函电(2)

Thank you very much for your hospitality in allowing me to stay overnight with you on my recent trip. It was a wonderful opportunity for us to catch up on many things. I was glad to experience a part of your relaxed life.

Rest assured that the remainder of the trip was a success, thanks in no small part to the good time I had with you and your family. I hope will be able to reciprocate when you visit China.

I am sending you some photos I took of you.

Words and Expressions

1. stay overnight 住宿
2. catch up on many things 追赶上一些事，了解近况
3. rest assured that 放心，因为……请安心
4. relaxed 放松的，轻松的
5. remainder 剩余的
6. in no small part 非常，十分
7. reciprocate 互换；回报

2-3 出差归来的感谢函电(3)

I am back at the office since yesterday, everything went well, seminars & workshops and flights!

I hope everyone is fine at Agai Trading Corporation. Please tell hello and thank you very much for everything to all of you. Best regards from Basel to all of you, and thanks again for the nice hospitality! About the picture of me in your homepage I think that is ok, I do like that. Hope to see you in September.

Words and Expressions

1. seminar 研讨会
2. workshop 专题讨论会
3. Basel 巴塞尔（瑞士西北部城市）
4. hospitality 招待，款待

小知识 **Agai Trading Corporation(アガイ商事株式会社)**

Agai Trading Corporation是位于日本东京的一家国际贸易公司，主营业务欧洲进口的高端摄影器材在日本的销售，是瑞士布朗摄影器材制造公司产品在日本的总代理。此公司有中国籍和加拿大籍员工，并在北京创建了大型摄影工作室，为在北京的全球专业摄影师提供瑞士布朗摄影器材的租赁业务。

2-4 访问工厂

Thank you very much for giving me the opportunity to visit your factory recently. I was impressed with your state-of-the-art equipment, and I found my visit very educational.

Please convey my appreciation to your staff, who made my trip both pleasant and rewarding. Thank you again for this valuable opportunity.

Words and Expressions

1. be impressed with 留下深刻的印象
2. state-of-the-art equipment 最先进的设备
3. educational 有教育意义的
4. convey 传达
5. rewarding 值得的

2-5 对能够来见面而致谢

Thank you very much for meeting with me last Wednesday. I enjoyed getting acquainted with you and your company. What I have learned from the meeting will certainly help me serve you better in the future. Please let me know if I can be of any assistance to you. Thank you.

Words and Expressions

1. get acquainted with 认识，了解
2. serve 服务
3. assistance 帮助

2-6 住宿招待(1)

Thank you so much for the warm hospitality you showed to our daughter Xiaofang. She must have enjoyed the visit very much; she won't let a day go by without talking about your family and the school. We are very happy and grateful that she had such a positive experience in your country.

Xiaofang will be writing to you soon. In the meantime, please accept our thanks. We hope there will be an opportunity for us to return your kindness soon.

Words and Expressions

1. warm hospitality 热情的款待
2. go by （时间）过去，流逝
3. grateful 感激的
4. apositive 积极的，肯定的，正面的
5. return your kindness 对你的善意感恩、回报

2-7　住宿招待(2)

We are very happy to have heard from WANG Xiaogang that he is really enjoying his stay in your home. We thank you so much for the kindness shown to him. We were somewhat concerned about his English speaking and listening ability, but he says that it has not been a problem, thanks to your patience. Please do not hesitate to tell him what the rules and expectations are in your home.

Thank you again for the wonderful things you are doing for WANG Xiaogang.

Words and Expressions

1. somewhat 有点,稍微
2. be concerned about 关切,关心
3. ability 能力,资格
4. patience 耐心
5. hesitate 犹豫

2-8　住宿招待(3)

One week has passed since I returned from England, but my mind is still there with you. Of course, it is nice to be back with my family and all my friends. But I do miss your family and the school.

Right now, I am working hard to get readjusted to life here. Once I am settled, I will write you more about how I am doing.

Thank you very much for everything you did to make my stay in your country so enjoyable. Please take care of yourselves.

Words and Expressions

1. my mind is still there with you 好像还和你们在一起
2. do miss 非常想念, do 表示强调
3. get readjusted to 重新调整到……,重新习惯……
4. be settled 安顿好

2-9　寄来的礼物

How thoughtful of you to send us the beautiful place mats for our wedding. Your good taste shows in the fine choice you made, and they fit just right with our decor. Your gift will long remind us of your friendship.

Thank you again, and we do hope you will be able to visit us in the near future.

Words and Expressions

1. how thoughtful of you to 你想得多么周到
2. place mat 桌垫
3. wedding 婚礼
4. fit 适合
5. decor 装饰
6. remind 提醒

2-10 出席高尔夫招待

This is just a quick note to let you know how much I enjoyed playing golf with you last week at Bubble Beach. The course was great with its challenging fairways.

Thank you again for the wonderful opportunity to share this relaxing day on the course.

Words and Expressions

1. a quick note 短信
2. challenging 挑战
3. fairways （高尔夫球场上的）平坦球道
4. relaxing 放松的
5. share 分享

2-11 参加宴会招待

Thank you very much for inviting my wife and me to the 125th anniversary of your company. We thoroughly enjoyed the party. It was indeed an honor to be invited to this event.

Thank you again.

Words and Expressions

1. anniversary 周年纪念
2. thoroughly 彻底的
3. indeed 的确
4. honor to be invited 很荣幸被邀请
5. event 活动

2-12 出席晚会

It was good to see you and your wife at our party the other day. You are our valued customer, and we were most pleased that you could attend. We hope you enjoyed meeting everyone there.

Once again, thank you for taking the time to come.

Words and Expressions

1. the other day 前几天
2. valued customer 重要的客户
3. attend 出席
4. take the time to come 花时间来

2-13 祝贺升职(1)

Thank you very much for your support and kind words upon my being appointed Chairperson of the board of Transpacific Shipping Company.

I will do my best to fulfill the obligations of this position, but by myself, success will be limited. Therefore, your continued friendship and guidance will be sought and appreciated.

Words and Expressions

1. be appointed Chairperson 被任命为主席
2. board 董事会
3. fulfill the obligation 履行职责
4. position 位置
5. by myself 仅仅靠我一个人
6. continued 持续的
7. guidance 指导

2-14 祝贺升职(2)

I heard the wonderful news that you have been promoted to the position of vice president at Bap Corporation. You have my heartfelt congratulations on this well-deserved promotion. There is no doubt you will have the same success in your new position as you had in your previous one.

Be assured that I welcome the increased opportunity to do business with you in the future.

Words and Expressions

1. be promoted to the position of... 晋升到……职位
2. vice president 副总经理
3. heartfelt congratulation 衷心的祝贺
4. well-deserved 应得的,当之无愧的
5. no doubt 毫无疑问
6. previous one (previous position) 前一个的(以前的职位)
7. be assured that 确信,坚信

2-15 祝贺获奖

I was delighted to learn that you have been named "outstanding journalist of the year". I can think of no one else who deserves it more and am very proud of you. Congratulations for all your achievements that merited this award.

I believe that this public recognition will contribute to elevating the industry standard, and I wish you many more years of continued success.

Words and Expressions

1. be delighted to learn 很高兴知道
2. be named 被选为
3. deserve 应获得的
4. outstanding journalist of the year 年度杰出新闻工作者
5. merit 值得,应得
6. award 奖
7. public recognition 公认
8. contribute to 有助于
9. elevate the industry standard 提高行业水准

2-16 祝贺新工厂落成

We are very happy to hear of the completion of your new factory in Dallas, Texas. We believe that this new facility will be the answer to the ever-increasing demand for your products.

My staff joins me in sending you our warmest congratulations on this happy occasion.

31

Words and Expressions

1. completion 完成
2. facility 设施
3. Dallas, Texas 达拉斯市,德克萨斯州（美国南方第一大都会,也是 1963 年美国第 35 任总统约翰·菲茨杰拉德·肯尼迪被暗杀事件发生地）
4. ever-increasing demand 不断增长的需求
5. on this happy occasion 在这个快乐的时刻

2–17 祝贺工厂建成 100 年

What an accomplishment to have successfully been in business for 100 years! This is surely a tribute to the fine products you have provided your customers over the past century.

Congratulations on a job well done. I wish you continued success for many years to come.

Words and Expressions

1. accomplishment 业绩
2. be in business 经营
3. tribute 体现,赞赏
4. over the past century 过去的一个世纪,过去的一百年
5. for many years to come 今后的许多年

2–18 致帮助就业的人

Thank you very much for providing the letter of reference. You wrote such a positive letter that I had to look twice to make sure you were speaking of me.

I am happy to tell you that thanks to your letter, I will start working next month. This is my dream job which I have been waiting for a long time. Thank you so much for your part in helping me achieve my goal.

Words and Expressions

1. letter of reference 推荐书
2. positive 积极的,正面的
3. achieve my goal 实现我的目标

2-19 致提供信息的人

Thanks for your recipe for stuffed mushrooms. I tried it and it was a big success. The mushrooms were just delicious. Thank you again.

Words and Expressions

1. recipe 食谱
2. mushroom 蘑菇
3. delicious 美味,好吃

2-20 致演讲的人

Thank you very much for the excellent speech at our monthly meeting last week. It was most motivational and received a positive response from the audience.

Thanks to your participation, the meeting was a great success.

Words and Expressions

1. motivational 动力,刺激
2. response 反响,反应
3. audience 观众
4. participation 参与

2-21 发晚了的感谢信

Though belated, please accept my gratitude for inviting me to lunch last month. The restaurant was wonderful! I am sorry not to have written sooner to express my appreciation for your hospitality.

I look forward to returning your kindness in the near future.

Words and Expressions

1. though belated 虽然来得迟了一点
2. gratitude 感激
3. express my appreciation 表达我的谢意

Exercise

Ⅰ. Fill in the blanks with the following words.

time	kindness	share	stay	hospitality
dream	kindness	thoughtful	participation	hesitate

1. Thank you again for the wonderful opportunity to _____ this relaxing day on the course.

2. How _____ of you to send us the beautiful place mats for our wedding.

3. Thank you very much for your _____ in allowing me to stay overnight with you on my recent trip.

4. Once again, thank you for taking the _____ to come.

5. We hope there will be an opportunity for us to return your _____ soon.

6. Thanks to your _____, the meeting was a great success.

7. We are very happy to have heard from David that he is really enjoying his _____ in your home.

8. This is my _____ job which I have been waiting for a long time.

9. We thank you so much for the _____ shown to him.

10. Please do not _____ to tell him what the rules and expectations are in your home.

Ⅱ. Translate the following words and phrases.

Section A: Translate into English.

1. 热情招待

2. 转达谢意

3. 出差

4. 接受感谢

5. 心意的工作

Section B: Translate into Chinese.

1. a positive experience

2. in the meantime

3. the excellent speech

4. warmest congratulations

5. appreciation

Ⅲ. Writing in English.

请给你的朋友写一封升职祝贺信。

3 Invitation
邀请函

> **Aims to Obtain**
>
> **Upon completion of the unit, you should:**
> - know how to write various official invitaions;
> - be able to make good use of the words or expressions to reply a general invitation.

3-1 晚宴正式邀请(1)

Mr. and Mrs. YUKIO TANAKA

Request the pleasure of your company

For cocktails and dinner

Saturday, the fourth of July

At seven o'clock

11-3 Kamiya-suji

Bunkyo-ku, TOKYO

The favor of a reply is requested.

Words and Expressions

1. request the pleasure of 恭请,恭候光临
2. company 除了公司的意思外,还有(社交)集会,聚会之意,在这表示出席聚会的意思
3. cocktails 鸡尾酒
4. favor 欢心;好感;宠爱;关切

3-2 晚宴正式邀请(2)

To celebrate the 30th anniversary of ABC Chemicals, the Board of Directors requests the honor of your presence at a reception to be held at the Royal Plaza Hotel in JIEFANGBEI, CHONGQING, beginning at 6:00 p.m, June 18, 2019.

The program will feature Dr. WANG MINGGANG as the keynote speaker. The occasion is formal, and dark suits and ties are required.

We request the favor of a reply.

Words and Expressions

1. 30th anniversary 30周年纪念日
2. the Board of Directors 董事会
3. presence 出席
4. reception 接待；欢迎
5. feature 以……为号召物，邀请……作重要角色
6. the keynote speaker 主讲人
7. the occasion is formal 正式场合
8. request the favor of a reply 期待关心与答复

3-3 收到邀请函

Thank you very much for the kind invitation to the banquet in honor of your new president, Mr. Heathrow. We would be most honored to attend this function, and look forward to seeing you there.

Words and Expressions

1. banquet 宴会
2. in honor of 为庆祝，为了向……表示敬意
3. be most honored to 非常荣幸（这里的most与very同义）
4. attend 参加
5. function 庆典，活动

3-4 拒绝邀请

Thank you for your kind invitation to the reception in celebration of the opening of your new factory. I extend to you my congratulations. Unfortunately, I will be unable to attend the event because of a prior commitment.

My colleagues and I send our best wishes for your continued success.

Words and Expressions

1. reception 接待
2. extend 发出（邀请、欢迎等）
3. in celebration of 庆贺
4. unfortunately 不幸的
5. prior commitment 优先承诺
6. colleague 同事

3-5 派对邀请(1)

My husband and I would like to invite you and your wife to a small dinner party at our home on February 16th. We hope that you can join us around seven p.m.. There will be a few other friends attending as well.

We look forward to seeing you then.

Words and Expressions

1. around seven p.m. 下午7点左右
2. as well 也

3-6 派对邀请(2)

We're having a party! David will be ten years old on May 15, and we want you to help us celebrate. We'll be having cake, ice cream and lots of surprises.

Please call me by April 30 if you plan to come. We look forward to seeing you soon.

Words and Expressions

1. celebrate 庆祝
2. surprise 惊喜

3-7 开业典礼邀请

We are pleased to have the opportunity to invite you to our open house on November 21st from 3:00 p.m. to 6:00 p.m. Please stop by at your convenience to meet us in our new office. Bring your friends and associates for wine and cheese.

We look forward to seeing you at 1136 SHATTUCK AVENUE, Berkeley (one block west of Oxford street).

Words and Expressions

1. open house 家庭招待会
2. stop by 顺便走访
3. at your convenience 在您方便的时候
4. associates 朋友;非正式会员
5. cheese 奶酪

3-8　邀请参加结婚典礼

We are very pleased to invite you to the wedding of our daughter, MAYUMI, to Thomas Chang, on May 15, 2019. The ceremony will be held at Saint John's Lutheran Church in AOYAMA at 2:00 p.m. followed by a reception at Yamate Country Club.

We hope that you will be able to join us for this very happy occasion.

Words and Expressions

1. ceremony 仪式
2. followed by a reception 接下来的招待宴会

3-9　参加结婚典礼的回信

My husband and I are thrilled to hear about your wedding plans. Please accept our heartfelt congratulations and best wishes to you both.

Thank you for including us among your guests on this happy occasion. We will, of course, be more than happy to attend your wedding and look forward to meeting Clifford on September 17.

Words and Expressions

1. be thrilled to 激动不已
2. heartfelt congratulations 发自内心的祝福
3. more than happy 无比高兴

3-10　邀请参加公司活动(1)

It is with great pleasure that we invite you to our 125th anniversary celebration on April 29, 2019, at Radasion Hotel in Guangzhou. The reception will begin at 6:00 p.m., and be followed by dinner.

We would be greatly honored if you could celebrate this occasion with us. RSVP by March 30.

Words and Expressions

1. with great pleasure 非常高兴
2. be greatly honored 很荣幸,不胜感激
3. RSVP 来自法语的 repondez sil vous plait,意为:请一定给个答复

3-11 邀请参加公司活动(2)

Trend International Co., Ltd is pleased to announce its 5th Annual Golf Tournament, to be held on August 18 at Bubble Beach Golf Course, Tampa, Florida. We would like to invite you to participate in the tournament.

Please call me at (813)555-5555 to reserve your place now. Reservations are limited, so please call early!

We look forward to seeing you there.

Words and Expressions

1. Co., Ltd. Company Limited 的缩写,即有限责任公司与股份有限公司的总称
2. announce 宣布,通知
3. annual 每年的
4. participate in 参加
5. tournament 比赛,锦标赛,联赛
6. reserve your place 预约你的席位

3-12 邀请参加展销会

We, at NAPA SCALE CO., LTD., would like to invite you to the International Scales Exposition scheduled from November 25 through November 30, at the Convention Center in LAS Vegas.

Please visit our booth, where you will be able to view models of all our products, including our latest F-4 model. We will be on hand to greet you and answer any questions you may have. We look forward to seeing you there.

Words and Expressions

1. Exposition 博览会,简写为 Expo
2. schedule from...through... 安排,预定计划从……到……
3. Convention Center 会议中心
4. LAS Vegas 拉斯维加斯(美国内华达州城市,闻名全球的赌城)
5. booth 展销会上的展位
6. latest 最新的
7. on hand 在现场
8. greet 欢迎,迎接,问候,恭候

> 小知识

Las Vegas

拉斯维加斯(Las Vegas)是美国中西部内华达州最大的城市,也是座享有极高国际声誉的世界四大赌城之一。从一个不起眼的破落村庄,到一座巨大的国际城市,拉斯维加斯只用了十年。它拥有"世界娱乐之都"和"结婚之都"的美称,是一座以赌博业为中心的旅游、购物、度假的世界知名度假城市。每年来拉斯维加斯旅游的3 890万旅客中,来购物和享受美食的占了大多数,专程来赌博的只占少数。2014年,拉斯维加斯成为全球最多新婚夫妇选择的蜜月旅行目的地。

如果你穷困潦倒还剩下几美元,去拉斯维加斯也许会咸鱼翻个身。如果你钱多花不完,去拉斯维加斯也许会体会到流浪汉的潇洒。拉斯维加斯就是这样,一面是地狱,一面是天堂。

拉斯维加斯会议展览中心(Las Vegas Convention Center)是目前世界上最繁忙最先进的多功能场馆之一。位于拉斯维加斯山谷的中心地带,拥有320万平方英尺的展览大厅,可容纳十万人以上,展览中心以其多功能性闻名于世。会展中心在步行距离内提供1.8万间客房,在3英里范围内提供5万间客房。一个豪华的休息厅及登记处连接现有的展厅、预计修建的展厅和会议室,这使得展览中心可以随意调整场地以适应多种会展需求。

3-13 回复邀请(1)

Thank you very much for your kind invitation. We are delighted to accept your invitation. Your wedding anniversary is also an important occasion for us and we'll surely come to your party to celebrate it. We haven't seen you both for several years and we miss you very much. We'll come to the party at half past six that evening, and look forward to it with pleasure.

> Words and Expressions

1. wedding anniversary 结婚纪念日
2. an important occasion 重要的场合,重要的日子,重要的时刻

3-14 回复邀请(2)

My wife and I are going to have a small dancing party to celebrate our 10th wedding anniversary. It is a very important occasion for us and we are going to invite some old friends and hope you two can come and join us. The party will be held at Room 168, Park Hotel, Culture Road at seven o'clock the next Saturday evening, December 10.

I know you have been busy recently, but I do hope you can manage it. We are looking forward to your coming with great pleasure.

Words and Expressions

1. recently 最近
2. manage 安排
3. with great pleasure 非常高兴，非常荣幸

3-15 邀请参加会议

Kind Reminder：

The seminar on "How to win Market by Wechat" is going to be held on Thursday(tomorrow)16:00 - 17:40, 7th of March 2019 at the Netherlands Consulate General in Chongqing, Unit 5404 - 05, Yingli International Financial Center. If you unfortunately cannot attend the event, please inform us by today.

Thank you very much in advance for your cooperation and look forward to meeting you soon!

Nicole from the European Chamber.

Words and Expressions

1. seminar 研讨会
2. win market 赢得市场
3. Wechat 微信
4. the Netherlands Consulate General in Chongqing 荷兰驻重庆领事馆
5. Yingli International Financial Center 英利国际金融中心
6. European Chamber 欧盟商会

3-16 邀请参加商务交流会

The European Chamber Southwest Chapter cordially invites you to a seminar to know more about doing business in Schleswig-Holstein (Germany) on the 29th November (Firday) 2019, at Kempinski Hotel Chongqing.

This seminar is co-organised with Mikro Partner Strategy Consulting and the Economy and Technology Promotion Center of Schleswig-Holstein, Germany. You will learn knowledge about Schleswig-Holstein region as well as consulting and support to Chinese companies who are interested in starting business there. It also provides a good opportunity for 10 to 15 guests to talk in depth with the officials and professionals face to face. Your online registration is valid only if a confirmation E-mail is received from us.

Words and Expressions

1. cordially 诚挚的
2. Kempinski Hotel 凯宾斯基酒店(著名的德系酒店)
3. co-organise 联合组织,联合举办
4. region 区域
5. talk in depth 深入交谈
6. online registration 在线注册
7. valid 有效的

小知识   **Kempinski Hotel(凯宾斯基酒店)**

凯宾斯基酒店是世界上历史悠久的豪华酒店集团,由德国人伯托·凯宾斯基(Berthold Kempinski)最初建立于1897年。酒店集团创建于德国,现旗下酒店遍布欧洲、中东、非洲、美洲和亚洲,在北京、重庆、柏林、布达佩斯、伊斯坦布尔、德累斯顿和日内瓦等34个目的地拥有76家豪华酒店和度假村。

凯宾斯基拥有历史悠久的地标性项目、城市生活方式酒店、豪华度假村,以及酒店式公寓,每家酒店均秉承凯宾斯基品牌的传统,让客人感受目的地文化风情。

3-17 邀请参加时装秀

We are pleased to invite you to join us in celebrating the 2019 Danish Fashion and Design Show in Chongqing, with exclusive products from KOPENHAGEN FUR and Liudu Fur.

The Royal Danish Consulate General in Chongqing have invited the Chinese famous fashion writer Ms. Li Mengsu to share with distinguished guests about the in-depth view of Danish fur design. During and after the fashion show it will be possible to purchase products from the participating brands. Please join us.

Words and Expressions

1. exclusive 专业的,专门的
2. KOPENHAGEN FUR 哥本哈根皮草
3. The Royal Danish Consulate General in Chongqing 丹麦王国驻重庆总领事馆
4. distinguished guests 尊敬的来宾
5. purchase 购买
6. the participating brands 参展品牌

3-18　邀请参加圣诞晚会

We are delighted to invite you to attend 2019 Chongqing Inter-Chamber Christmas Party which is to be held on 2nd December, Monday 2019 at Crowne Plaza Chongqing City Centre. The event includes dinner drinks, a big Christmas dinner of a set 4 course festive western dinner, live music, lucky draw and much more! There will also be a children's room with food managed by Song Ching Ling Kindergarten.

Time：2nd December 2019, Monday, 18:00 - 22:00 hrs

Venue：6th Floor, Crowne Plaza Chongqing City Centre, 31 Zhongfu Road

Words and Expressions

1. festive 喜庆的；欢乐的；节日的
2. live music 现场音乐表演
3. lucky draw 幸运抽奖
4. Venue 会场

3-19　邀请参加会员专属晚宴

All the members of the European Chamber Southwest Chapter are invited to a members' VIP dinner on the 28th November 2019 to learn a briefing from the Chairman of Southwest Chapter Mr. Paul Sives about the Chamber's recent European Tour that took place in the last week of September in Brussels. Dinner is held at Boardroom 4F, Regent Hotel Chongqing.

Words and Expressions

1. VIP 贵宾,大人物,Very Important People 的缩写
2. Briefing 简要情况汇报
3. take place 发生,举行
4. Brussels 布鲁塞尔(比利时首都)
5. Boardroom 董事会厅

3-20　邀请参加商务速配

We are delighted to invite you to the 5th Speed Business Meeting on the 20th December 2019. Join us for an exciting evening to expand your business and social connections and to meet possible partners and customers in a fast way!

During the event you will have the opportunity to strike up quick conversations with many people, and introduce yourself and the business profile of the company you represent. At the end of the event we provide a short networking session which allows you to further develop the newly formed business connections and have a friendly chat with the participants.

It also provides a great opportunity for you to jump out of your knowledge and learn new business models in other areas in this rapid developing environment. Please bring along some small gifts for your counterparts for the Christmas.

Words and Expressions

1. expand 扩大
2. social connections 社会关系，社交人脉
3. strike up 建立起
4. profile 简介
5. session 阶段
6. jump out of your knowledge 开阔视野，增长见识
7. in this rapid developing environment 在这个快速发展的环境下
8. counterparts 同仁

Exercise

Ⅰ. Fill in the blanks with the following words.

| pleasure | heartfelt | depth | stop | advance |
| occasion | valid | among | attend | bring |

1. Please accept our _____ congratulations and best wishes to you both.
2. Thank you for including _____ us your guests on this happy occasion.
3. It also provides a good opportunity for 10 to 15 guests to talk in _____ with the officials and professionals face to face.
4. Your online registration is _____ only if a confirmation E-mail is received from us.
5. It is a very important _____ for us and we are going to invite some old friends and hope you two can come and join us.
6. We are looking forward to your coming with great _____.
7. Please _____ by at your convenience to meet us in our new office.
8. _____ your friends and associates for wine and cheese.
9. If you unfortunately cannot _____ the event, please inform us by today.
10. Thanks very much in _____ for your cooperation and look forward to meeting you soon!

Ⅱ. **Translate the following words and phrases.**

Section A：Translate into English.

1. 邀请函

2. 会员专属晚宴

3. 公司周年庆

4. 商务速配

5. 结婚典礼

Section B：Translate into Chinese.

1. a small dancing party

2. convenience

3. rapid developing environment

4. attend the event

5. Danish Fashion and Design Show

Ⅲ. **Writing in English.**

请给你的客户写一封参加公司开业活动邀请函。

4 Reservation
预约函

> **Aims to Obtain**
>
> **Upon completion of the unit, you should：**
>
> • grasp some basic tactics about reservation;
>
> • know how to write letters related to cancel an appointment or reservation;
>
> • know how to make a request or refuse request about an appointment.

4-1 海外旅行时顺便拜访

I am going to be traveling in England this summer, and I would very much like to see you if possible.

I am scheduled to arrive in London on July 30, and will be until August 6 at the Hotel St. Francis. Please let me know what sort of plans you might have.

I am very excited about my trip and about seeing you.

Words and Expressions

1. be scheduled to 定于，计划于
2. sort of 种类
3. excited 兴奋的

4-2　对拜访的回复

How nice to hear that you plan to visit Singapore next month and that you will be able to take some time to see me.

The best time for me to get together with you would be on the evening of Friday, July 5th. Please tell me the address and phone number of where you will be staying.

I am eagerly looking forward to seeing you.

Words and Expressions

1. take some time 花些时间
2. get together with you 和你在一起
3. eagerly 渴望地；热切地

4-3　机场迎接请求

This is to confirm that Mr. Zhang Tao will arrive at New York International Airport at 10:30 a.m. October 28, 2019 on Air China Flight #136.

Will you kindly meet him at the airport upon arrival? Mr. Zhang will be carrying a brown umbrella. Your assistance will be very much appreciated.

Words and Expressions

1. confirm 确认
2. Air China 中国国际航空
3. Flight #136 136号航班
4. upon arrival 在到达时
5. will be carrying a brown umbrella 将拿着一把棕色的伞

4-4　面谈申请(1)

Your name came to my attention recently in my search for experts in the field of computer viruses. I would like to meet with you to discuss the possibility of a joint venture.

Could I visit you during the first week of June? I believe there is potential for a mutually beneficial relationship.

Enclosed is my resume. I look forward to your early reply. Thank you very much.

Words and Expressions

1. came to my attention 引起了我的注意
2. experts 专家
3. in the field of 在这一领域
4. viruses 病毒
5. joint venture 合资企业
6. potential 潜在的
7. mutually beneficial relationship 互利互惠关系
8. resume 简历

4-5 面谈申请(2)

It was a pleasure to meet you at the Pacific Rim Trade Symposium on June 5, 2019. I enjoyed talking with you even though it was rather brief. I was impressed with your in-depth knowledge of China's economy.

I would welcome an opportunity to get to know you better—perhaps over lunch. Please call if you are interested in scheduling such a meeting. Thank you.

Words and Expressions

1. Pacific Rim Trade 环太平洋贸易
2. Symposium 研讨会,论坛
3. even though 即使
4. brief 短暂的,简短
5. in-depth knowledge 深入了解

4-6 接受面谈申请

I received your letter of April 18, 2019, indicating your interest in meeting me. I would be happy to see you June 4 from 9:00 a.m. to 10:00 a.m. in my office at the research center. If you could send me a synopsis of your proposals prior to our meeting, it would be helpful.

I look forward to meeting with you on June 4, unless I hear from you to the contrary.

Words and Expressions

1. indicating 指示,显示
2. synopsis 概要
3. proposals 提案
4. prior to 提前,在……之前
5. unless 除非
6. to the contrary 与之相反的(变更)

4-7 通知与代理面谈

Thank you for your letter of April 4, indicating your interest in meeting me regarding our new product. Unfortunately, I have a scheduling conflict that day and will be unable to meet you. I have passed your letter on to my assistant. She will be waiting for your arrival that day.

Words and Expressions

1. a scheduling conflict 时间冲突(计划冲突)
2. pass your letter on to my assistant 把你的信交给我的助手

4-8 拒绝面谈(1)

I received your letter of April 18, 2019, requesting a meeting with me regarding your company's insurance programs.

However, as I do not see any need to discuss the matter at this time, I wish to decline your request. Should the situation change in the future, however, I will contact you. I am sorry we could not take you up on your kind offer.

Words and Expressions

1. insurance programs 保险项目
2. decline 删除,取消
3. should the situation change 如果情况有变(虚拟语气)
4. contact you 联系你(注意 you 之前不要加 to 或 with 等助词)
5. take sb. up on sth. 接受或采纳某人的某事

4-9 拒绝面谈(2)

Thank you for your letter of April 18, 2019, indicating an interest in meeting with me.

Unfortunately, I will be out of town just at the time you are in the area, and therefore will be unable to see you. If you are interested in meeting at some future date, please do not hesitate to contact me again.

I am sorry I am unable to accommodate your request this time.

Words and Expressions

1. out of town 出差(on business)
2. therefore 因此,所以
3. do not hesitate to 不要犹豫,不要客气
4. accommodate your request 满足你的要求

4-10 预约面谈

I am writing to ask a favor. Gary Clark, our vice president, and I wish to visit AMP Instruments Inc. in September to discuss future business. I have tried several times to schedule a meeting with them, but without success to date.

Would you kindly contact the above mentioned firm locally and arrange an appointment to meet with their president? We will be available for such a meeting during the second week of September.

Thank you for your assistance.

Words and Expressions

1. ask a favor 请帮个忙
2. above mentioned firm 上面提到的公司
3. without success to date 到目前为止都没成功
4. assistance 支持,帮助
5. be available 有空,方便

4-11 预约确认和取消

This is to confirm our appointment made by telephone for Thursday, May 9, 2019 at 10:00 a.m. in the lobby of the Forum Hotel in Los Angeles. In case of any change, please contact me at (213)555-0101.

I am looking forward to seeing you.

Words and Expressions

1. confirm our appointment 确认我们的预约
2. lobby 大堂

3. In case of 在……情况下，如果……

4-12 参观申请

I would like to request permission to visit your water treatment research center on the morning of April 27, 2019. I would be grateful if you could arrange a tour of the facilities for me at that time.

If at all possible, a brief opportunity to talk with a key staff member would be most appreciated.

Enclosed is a short description of my background. Please let me know if you have any questions or need additional information regarding my request.

I look forward to receiving your permission, and thank you for your cooperation.

Words and Expressions

1. permission 许可
2. water treatment research center 水疗研究中心
3. facilities 设备
4. If at all possible 如果可能
5. brief 短时间的，简单的
6. a key staff member 干部
7. enclosed is... 同信附上的是……
8. description 描述
9. background 背景（经历）

4-13 答应参观申请

We are happy to accommodate your request to visit our facilities. We will be expecting you Saturday, April 27, 2019 at 10:00 a.m., as specified in your letter. Upon arrival, please ask for Mr. Honda at the public relations reception desk. He will arrange a brief tour and a time for questions and answers.

If there are any questions that you need to have answered before your visit, please do not hesitate to contact me.

Words and Expressions

1. accommodate 满足，答应
2. as specified in your letter 如信中具体指出的
3. reception desk 接待处
4. Upon arrival 在到达之后

5. a brief tour 一个短暂的参观

6. hesitate 犹豫

7. please do not hesitate to contact me 请不要客气与我联系（惯用语，结束客套语）

4-14 拒绝参观申请

Thank you for your letter of November 1, expressing your interest in visiting our central lab. Unfortunately, due to our company's new policy, our facilities are temporarily closed to the public.

We are sorry we cannot accommodate your request at this time. However, if you specify your needs and interests, we may be able to suggest other labs. Please do not hesitate to write to us.

Words and Expressions

1. express 表达
2. lab 研究所（laboratory 的缩写）
3. due to 因为
4. temporarily 暂时的
5. closed to the public 对公众关闭
6. accommodate 帮忙
7. specify 明确提出，详细说明

Exercise

Ⅰ. Fill in the blanks with the following words.

| assistant | discuss | up | available | attention |
| change | arrival | arrange | firm | conflict |

1. Your name came to my _____ recently in my search for experts in the field of computer viruses.
2. I would like to meet with you to _____ the possibility of a joint venture.
3. Would you kindly contact the above mentioned _____ locally and arrange an appointment to meet with their president?
4. We will be _____ for such a meeting during the second week of September.
5. Unfortunately, I have a scheduling _____ that day and will be unable to meet you.
6. I have passed your letter on to my _____.

7. Upon _____ , please ask for Mr. Honda at the public relations reception desk.

8. He will _____ a brief tour and a time for questions and answers.

9. Should the situation _____ in the future, however, I will contact you.

10. I am sorry we could not take you _____ on your kind offer.

Ⅱ. Translate the following words and phrases.

Section A：Translate into English.

1. 预约确认

2. 早日答复

3. 探讨可能性

4. 参观申请

5. 公司新政策

Section B：Translate into Chinese.

1. a joint venture

2. accommodate

3. a mutually beneficial relationship

4. get to know

5. receiving your permission

Ⅲ. Writing in English.

请给你的客户写一封参观对方公司的申请函。

5　Notification
　　通　知

Aims to Obtain

Upon completion of the unit, you should：

- know how to write letters about announcement；
- be able to make good use of the words or expressions to write merger, new open, address and name change of company, etc.；
- grasp some basic tactics about writing negative announcement such resignation, price up.

5-1　新设通知

We Heiwa co., ltd. proudly announce that on october 1, 2019, we will be opening a new branch office in New York under the following name and address:

 Heiwa America lnc.
 46th st., New York, NY.
 Tel:(212)876-4566
 Fax:(212)876-4567
 Web site:www.eiwamec.com

This new office is being set up to facilitate business transactions between customers in the United States and our head office in Tokyo. Please stop by to visit our new facilities and meet the staff.

Words and Expressions

1. branch office 分公司
2. Inc. 股份有限公司（Incorporation 的缩写）
3. set up 设置
4. facilitate business transactions 使商业交易便利化
5. head office 总公司；总部
6. stop by 顺便走访
7. facilities 设施
8. staff 全体职员

5-2　搬迁通知

Please be advised that effective March 1, 2019, our address has been changed from 140 Redwood Drive, Riverside, CA92506 to 1010 Union Street, Apt.#300. New York, NY 1003

The new telephone number is (212)345-5678, and our E-mail address is ginfo@donaco.com. Please direct all the future correspondence to the new address. Thank you for your attention.

Words and Expressions

1. effective 有效的；起作用的
2. direct all the future correspondence to… 今后的所有信函直接寄到……
3. the new address 新地址
4. attention 关注，关心，注意

5-3　与其他公司合并通知

We are pleased to announce the merger of our company with Delta Trading Co., Ltd, Manila, as of April 1, 2019. The new company will be named Donghai Delta International with its head office at 1919—33 kangnam-ku, Seoul, Korea. As a result of this merger, we should be able to offer better sales service in our overseas markets.

We thank you for your past patronage, and look forward to even better relations with you in the future.

Words and Expressions

1. merger 合并
2. as of April 1, 2019 从 2019 年 4 月 1 日开始
3. head office 总部
4. as a result of 由于……的结果
5. overseas markets 海外市场
6. patronage 资助；赞助

5-4　公司名变更通知

Effective May 15, 2019, Foshan textile Co, Ltd. will become Foshan Pacific Tech Inc.. Our address and phone numbers will remain unchanged. This name change is being made to reflect the nature of business.

Thank you for your continued support of our business. We look forward to serving you even better as Pacific Tech.

Words and Expressions

1. remain unchanged 保持不变
2. reflect 反映；考虑
3. the nature of business 业务内容
4. continued support 继续支持

5-5　终止业务关系通知

Please be advised that Hutton Pet Food Company has recently been acquired by National Pets Network. In order to streamline our operations, it is necessary to terminate our business relationship with you as of the end of this month.

We regret taking this action, as your services have always been satisfactory.

Thank you for all your past business with us.

> **Words and Expressions**

1. be acquired by 被……收购
2. streamline 使……精简,使……合理
3. operations 经营
4. terminate 结束,终止
5. taking this action 采取这个行动,采取这个措施

5-6 工作调动通知

I am happy to inform you that as of April 1, 2019, I will be transferred from the Hawaii branch Office of Minato Bussan Co., Ltd. to its New York head office. My new position will be director of sales.

Mr. Smith will be my successor as manager of the Hawaii branch office. Thank you for your past patronage, and I ask that you continue the same with the new manager.

> **Words and Expressions**

1. be transferred from...to... 被从……调动到……
2. director of sales 销售总监
3. successor 接替的人,继任者
4. patronage 资助,赞助;光顾,惠顾
5. Hawaii branch office 夏威夷分公司

5-7 宣布公司新任

We at Jiatian food Co. Ltd., are happy to announce that Mr. Tian Guoqing has been chosen as our new president as of June 1. Mr. Tian Guoqing comes to us with a long history of success at former companies. Please join us in welcoming this new leader of our company.

> **Words and Expressions**

1. new president 新总裁;新董事
2. a long history of success 非常多的业绩
3. at former companies 在以前的公司

5-8　新任致辞

I would like to take this opportunity to inform you of my appointment as president of Cyberg Electronics. While this position entails a number of new responsibilties, with your support I am looking forward to this new challenge. Thank you for your continued business and your friendship.

I hope to have an early opportunity to meet with you.

Words and Expressions

1. entail 附带,需要;牵涉
2. responsibility 责任
3. with your support 在你们的支持下
4. challenge 挑战

5-9　辞职通知(1)

I have recently left my employment with Vanke Housing for personal reasons.

I plan to relax for a while to recuperate before I take up another job as a freelance editor. If you happen to know of any future openings, please let me know. Thank you for your continuing friendship.

Words and Expressions

1. left my employment 离开工作岗位,辞职
2. personal reasons 个人原因
3. recuperate 恢复;复原
4. take up another job 从事其他工作
5. a freelance editor 自由编辑

5-10　辞职通知(2)

Dear all,

Please be advised that I will work at Agai Trading Corp. till March 31, 2020.

My colleague, Miss Masae Okishima will continue to pick up all my business transaction with you.

I really appreciate for all your kind support during my service in the company and hope you can offer the same support to the company in the future. Thank you.

Words and Expressions

1. Corp. 公司（corporation 的缩写）
2. colleague 同事
3. pick up all my business transaction 接替我一切与你们的业务交易（工作）

5-11 客户回复辞职通知(3)

I'm so sorry I am too late, I hope this E-mail will reach you anyway.

I wanted to send you all my best wishes for your future and thank you for all your help when I was at your company.

Best regards from Switzerland.

Words and Expressions

1. reach 到达，通知到
2. Switzerland 瑞士

5-12 退出协会通知

With much regret, I am leaving the Lions Club effective July 31, 2019. This decision was not easy to make as I have thoroughly enjoyed my association with fellow members during the past seven years. However, due to my age and deteriorating health, there was no other choice.

Please convey my deep appreciation to every member for their friendship. I will always remember the good times we have enjoyed.

Words and Expressions

1. With much regret 非常遗憾
2. effective 有效的
3. thoroughly 彻底地；完全地
4. association with 与……交流
5. fellow 同伴的；同事的；同类的；同情况的
6. deteriorating health 正在恶化的体质
7. convey my deep appreciation 深表谢意

5-13 涨价通知

Although we have tried to avoid taking this action, we must raise our prices by 7%, across the board effective August 1, 2019. This action is necessitated by the increased cost of raw materials and labor. We will, however, honor any orders at the current prices, as long as they are received on or before July 31, 2019.

We regret this necessity. We will, however, do our utmost to continue to serve you in the best possible way.

Words and Expressions

1. avoid 避免
2. taking this action 采取这项措施
3. across the board 一律，全体商品都包括在内
4. be necessitated by 因为……而必要的（措施）
5. the increased cost 成本上升
6. raw materials and labor 原材料和劳动力
7. honor any orders 遵守任何命令
8. necessity 必要性
9. do our utmost 尽我们最大的努力

5-14 寄送资料通知

Aloha motors plans to renovate its computer network in the office building at 556 central avenue, Yolo city by the end of 2019. Therefore, we would like to invite you to participate in the bid. The bid package will be mailed to you upon request. Your bid must be submitted to this office before October 18, 2019.

Thank you for your interest.

Words and Expressions

1. renovate 更新；修复
2. central avenue 中央大街
3. bid 投标
4. bid package 一整套投标资料
5. mail to you upon request 根据要求邮寄给你
6. submit 提交

5-15 寄送价格表通知

We thank you for your letter of April 30, 2019.

In accordance with your request, we are sending you a copy of our latest price list for your information.

As there is a heavy demand for the goods, we would suggest that you advise us by E-mail.

We look for forward to your early reply.

> Words and Expressions

1. In accordance with 根据……
2. a heavy demand 大量需求

5-16 不能按时交货通知

Owing to the problem at the port, we will not be able to meet the agreed delivery date of December 25, 2019. We are trying our best to make the goods reach you in time but the contracted date has now become unrealistic.

We are very sorry for any inconvenience that this may cause to you, but the delay is due to circumstances beyond our control.

> Words and Expressions

1. owing to the problem 由于……问题
2. port 港口
3. unrealistic 不切实际的
4. inconvenience 不方便的
5. inconvenience that this may cause to you 由此可能给你们带来的不便
6. circumstances 境况,境遇
7. beyond our control 远离我们的掌控,不在我们的控制下

5-17 关于公司重新装修的调查问卷

Questionnaire on Office Refurbishment

We are currently planning to refurbish the offices of International Trade Company. Could you complete this questionnaire so that your feelings are represented in our discussion with the Board?

1. How would you describe the present layout of furniture at International Trade Company?

Very Good	☐
Good	☐
Adequate	☐
Poor	☐

Very poor ☐

2. What do you think is the most important feature of good office furniture?

Comfortable ☐

Durable ☐

Attractive ☐

Function efficiently ☐

3. What image do you think we should project of our company?

Very Modern ☐

Traditional ☐

Simple and functional ☐

Extravagant ☐

Thank you for your cooperation. Please turn this questionnaire in to the Personnel Department before January 5, 2020.

Words and Expressions

1. questionnaire 问卷调查
2. refurbishment 整修；翻修
3. durable 持久的；耐用的
4. function efficiently 功能齐全，功能有效
5. layout 布局；安排
6. adequate 足够的；适当的
7. extravagant 过度的；奢侈的

5-18 订购报纸的内容通知

It's Your Newspaper

Business Weekly

CHINA DAILY

Published every Tuesday, *Business Weekly* carries in-depth reports about China's economic development, policies and environment for foreign investment, foreign trade and financial and market situation.

It features inside information and analysis of business events, as well as special columns contributed by China's most authoritative scholars and officials in economics.

Words and Expressions

1. environment for foreign investment 外资投资环境
2. analysis 分析
3. special columns 特殊专栏
4. contribute 投稿(给杂志等)
5. authoritative scholars 权威学者

5-19 支店成立公告

The president and directors of Nan Yang Investment Co. Ltd take the pleasure in announcing the official opening their Changjiang Branch at 15 Heping East Street on January 19, 2019 and request the pleasure of the company of all friends at a reception to be held on the same day and at the same place from 1:00 to 3:00 p.m..

Words and Expressions

1. directors 董事会
2. take the pleasure in announcing 非常高兴/荣幸地宣布
3. branch 支店

Exercise

Ⅰ. **Fill in the blanks with the following words.**

personal	reach	action	latest	merger
announce	patronage	demand	transaction	continue

1. We are pleased to _____ the merger of our company with Delta Trading Co,Ltd., Manila, as of April 1, 2019.
2. As a result of this _____, we should be able to offer better sales service in our overseas markets.
3. We thank you for your past _____, and look forward to even better relations with you in the future.
4. In accordance with your request, we are sending you a copy of our price _____ list for your information.
5. As there is a heavy _____ for the goods, we would suggest that you advise us by e mail.
6. I'm so sorry I am too late, I hope this E-mail will _____ you anyway.
7. My colleague, Miss Masae Okishima will continue to pick up all my business

_____ with you.

8. I have recently left my employment with Wanke Housing for _____ reasons.

9. Thank you for your past patronage, and I ask that you _____ the same with the new manager.

10. We regret taking this _____, as your services have always been satisfactory.

Ⅱ. Translate the following words and phrases.

Section A: Translate into English.

1. 公司新任

2. 支店

3. 宣布合并

4. 调查问卷

5. 涨价

Section B: Translate into Chinese.

1. take up another job

2. the current prices

3. new challenge

4. business events

5. Office Refurbishment

Ⅲ. Writing in English.

请为你的客户写一个公司名称变更通知。

6 Recommendation
介绍推荐函

Aims to Obtain

Upon completion of the unit, you should:
- know how to write letters about recommendation;
- be able to make good use of the words or expressions to write letter of reference, introduction, etc..

6-1　要求应聘者寄送信用查询书

We have received your application for the position of copywriter at tiger technical services. In order to complete your application, we require a letter of reference from your most recent employer. Please have the letter sent to my attention at the address above.

Words and Expressions

1. application 申请；请求
2. copywriter 打字员
3. a letter of reference 推荐书
4. employer 雇主；老板
5. attention 注意
6. at the address above 按照上面的地址

6-2　请求得到信用查询方的许可

We would like your permission to use your name as a reference in our application for membership in the international shippers association.

If you have an objection, please let us know by return mail. If we don't hear from you, we will assume your consent, and thank you for your cooperation.

Words and Expressions

1. reference 信用查询方
2. membership 会员资格；会员
3. international shippers association 国际托运协会
4. objection 反对
5. by return mail 寄回来
6. assume your consent 认为你同意

6-3　请求得到信用查询方给出信用查询书

Jefferey Cohen, one of your former employees, has applied for an engineering position in firm and gave me your name as a reference. Will you kindly comment on his ability to work with little supervision? Of course, we will keep your comments in the strictest confidence.

Thank you for your assistance.

Words and Expressions

1. former 以前的
2. employee 雇员
3. engineering position 工程师职位
4. firm 公司
5. comment 评论
6. supervision 监督；管理
7. strictest confidence 严格保密

6-4 推荐信委托

I hope you can remember me. I am a 2019 graduate of ACME Technical College, and am applying for the position of technical writer at XYZ Services.

May I ask if you would be kind enough to write a recommendation letter for me, and send it to the company at the following address?

  XYZ Services

  158 main street

  Anytown, ohio 12345

  Attention: Director of Human Resources

Thank you for your attention to this matter.

Words and Expressions

1. graduate 毕业生
2. recommendation 推荐
3. Director of Human Resources 人力资源部部长

6-5 介绍信委托

May I ask you a favor? I need a letter of introduction to Dr. Hart of the School of Business as the University of Toronto, and I would like to ask you to write one for me.

I am planning to visit the university to observe their M.B.A. Program, and I know your letter of introduction would be very helpful because of your association with the school. Would you please send your letter directly to Dr. Hart at your earliest convenience?

Thank you very much for your help.

Words and Expressions

1. May I ask you a favor? 我可以请你帮个忙吗？你可以帮我一下吗？
2. the School of Business 商学院
3. the University of Toronto 多伦多大学
4. observe 参观,考察,研究
5. M.B.A 工商管理硕士(Master of Business Administration 的缩写)
6. letter of introduction 介绍信
7. at your earliest convenience 在你最方便的时候

6-6 拒绝推荐委托

I have received your request for a recommendation letter for your research scholarship application. However, I am afraid that I do not feel qualified to write such a letter because I have too little knowledge of you.

I am sorry I cannot help you with this request, but I believe you will be able to find someone else who can help.

Words and Expressions

1. scholarship 奖学金
2. feel qualified to 有资格
3. have too little knowledge of you 对你不太了解

6-7 介绍信(1)

I have the pleasure of introducing Miss Wang Dongfang. I have known her as a former student as well as a good friend, for almost ten years. She has always impressed me with her keen interest in learning.

Miss Wang will be visiting your area next month. Would you kindly meet with her and offer any assistance that she may need? I know she would appreciate it very much. Thank you very much for your assistance.

Words and Expressions

1. impress 感动
2. keen 热心
3. keen interest in learning 对学习非常感兴趣
4. area 地区,区域

6-8 介绍信(2)

Jane shoemaker is currently seeking employment with your organization, and I would very much like to give her my endorsement.

I have known Jane for the past seven years as a business associate. She is a highly intelligent person with a warm personality. Her real strength lies in international marketing. Above all, she is a hard worker.

I strongly recommend Jane Shoemaker for the position. I know you will find her a valuable asset to your organization.

Words and Expressions

1. seek 寻找；追求
2. endorsement 保障，支持
3. business associate 同事
4. intelligent 聪明的
5. warm personality 温和的人格，人品
6. real strength 实际强项
7. Above all 除了以上还……，而且
8. valuable asset 贵重的财产，宝贵的人才

6-9 介绍信(3)

I would like to introduce our new district sales manager, Mr. Thomas Lu. His extensive marketing experience makes him a valuable addition to our firm.

Mr. Lu will contact you soon to schedule a meeting. I hope you will find him helpful in improving our service to you.

Thank you.

Words and Expressions

1. district sales manager 地区销售经理
2. extensive 广阔的；广大的；
3. a valuable addition 有价值的加入
4. schedule a meeting 安排会议
5. improve our service 提高我们的服务

6-10 介绍海外客户

This letter introduces to you one of our valued customers, Kudo optical

Co., Ltd..

Kudo optical is a well established engineering firm specializing in camera lenses. We have conducted business with this firm since 1970, and our relationship has always been most satisfactory. In particular, their strength lies in their superior level of technology.

We have no hesitation in recommending Kudo Optical as one of the best in the industry. If you need more information, please feel free to contact us.

Words and Expressions

1. optical 视觉的；视力的
2. camera lenses 照相机镜头
3. conduct 组织实施；实行
4. superior level of technology 领先的技术水平
5. have no hesitation 毫不犹豫
6. feel free to 不要客气

Exercise

Ⅰ. Fill in the blanks with the following words.

| experience | knowledge | recommendation |
| schedule | district | |

1. I have received your request for a _____ letter for your research scholarship application.
2. However, I am afraid that I do not feel qualified to write such a letter because I have too little _____ of you.
3. I would like to introduce our new _____ sales manager, Mr.Thomas Lu.
4. His extensive marketing _____ makes him a valuable addition to our firm.
5. Mr. Lu will contact you soon to _____ a meeting.

Ⅱ. Translate the following words and phrases.

Section A: Translate into English.

1. 推荐信
2. 信用查询书
3. 海外客户

Section B: Translate into Chinese.

1. superior level of technology

2. a letter of introduction
3. international marketing

7 Sale Promotion
推　销

> **Aims to Obtain**
> **Upon completion of the unit, you should:**
> - know how to write letters about sales promotion;
> - be able to make good use of the words or expressions to write establish business relations with your partner;
> - grasp some basic tactics about writing after-sale service, follow-up after fair.

7-1 推广预约

As the new regional sales manager for southern California, my first objective is to get acquainted with you and your company in order to serve you in the best possible way.

I will be in your area in the first week of June and would appreciate a few minutes of your time on Tuesday, June 4 to introduce myself. I will call in a few days to confirm my appointment.

Words and Expressions

1. regional sales manager 地区销售经理
2. objective 目标
3. confirm my appointment 确认我的预约

7-2 寻找推销契机

Stanford Biotech Inc. is a manufacturer of medical testing instruments. More than 30% of the hospitals and clinics in our country are our customers.

We are now extending our business to your country and are writing to you as a prospective customer. For your review, we have enclosed some brochures that introduce our products. Please let us know where your interests lie, and we will respond immediately. Thank you.

Words and Expressions

1. manufacturer 制造商
2. medical testing instruments 医疗检验仪器
3. clinics 诊所
4. extending our business 拓展我们的业务
5. prospective customer 潜在的顾客
6. for your review 供你参考
7. brochures 小册子
8. respond immediately 立刻回复

7-3 新品推广

We are introducing a new water softening system to the market. We believe that this product will meet the needs and tastes of individuals interested in healthy living.

Enclosed is our promotional literature giving you full details of the new product. You can take advantage of a special introductory sales price through October 31, 2019. We urge you not to pass up this opportunity.

Words and Expressions

1. water softening system 水软化系统
2. tastes of individuals 个人品位
3. healthy living 健康生活
4. promotional literature 宣传推广资料
5. take advantage of 利用(……的优惠)
6. special introductory sales price 新品销售特别价格
7. urge 催促，极力主张
8. pass up this opportunity 错过这次机会

7-4 服务亮点推销

Is your firm equipped with the work force to conduct business in foreign language? If your answer is "yes", disregard this letter. If not, please keep reading.

Multilingual Services Inc. provides excellent services in intercultural communication. In particular, our expertise lies in written translation of technical materials. Our services are prompt and cost-effective. Give us a try. You will be satisfied. We are enclosing a copy of our brochure and hope to have the opportunity to serve you. Thank you for your attention.

Words and Expressions

1. be equipped with 储备
2. work force 劳动力（人才）
3. multilingual 使用多种语言的
4. intercultural 不同文化间的
5. in particular 尤其，特别
6. expertise 专业人员；专家
7. cost-effective 高效益的，性价比高的

7-5 展会后的跟进

Thank you for your visit to our booth at the National Machine Tools Show held recently in Las Vegas. Our representatives enjoyed meeting you.

At the show, you indicated an interest in our fully-automated lathes. We are, therefore, sending by separate mail our "Trade Show Special" quotations.

We hope to hear from you soon.

Words and Expressions

1. booth 展位
2. representative 代表
3. indicate an interest in 对……表示出兴趣
4. fully-automated lathes 全自动车床
5. sending by separate mail 另外单独寄出
6. "Trade Show Special" quotations 展销会特别报价

7-6 售后服务

About a month ago, I sent you, in response to your request, our proposal for sales training for your employees. If you have had a chance to look over the program, I would like to know if you have some questions, or possibly have made your decision.

I will phone you around the middle of next week. I am looking forward to discussing your plans so that I can better serve you. Thank you.

Words and Expressions

1. in response to 对……做出的回应
2. proposal 建议

3. look over the program 查看一下计划安排
4. decision 决策
5. serve 服务

7-7　作为代理店的推销

We became acquainted with your products through the Pan American Trade Fair in New York and were impressed with your design concept.

As an import firm with expertise in fashion merchandising, we feel confident that we could successfully market your products in Taiwan.

Should you be interested in working with us, please contact us. In order to give you an overview of our company, I am enclosing a copy of our company profile. Thank you.

Words and Expressions

1. become acquainted with 知道,了解
2. Trade Fair 贸易展销会
3. design concept 设计理念
4. confident 自信,信心
5. overview 概况
6. company profile 公司简介

7-8　同意成为代理店申请

Thank you for your letter of April 29, 2018 offering to represent our products in China. We are very interested in your proposal and would like to meet with you. How does sometime early next month sound?

We are enclosing a copy of our company profile for your reference. Likewise, we would like as much information as possible about your firm in order to better prepare for this first meeting. We look forward to hearing from you soon.

Words and Expressions

1. represent our products 代理我们的产品
2. likewise 同样的,也;而且

7-9　拒绝代理申请

Thank you for your interest in representing our merchandise in your country. Unfortunately, we must decline your proposal this time since we already have an exclusive sales agent in India.

Thank you again for considering us.

Words and Expressions

1. decline 谢绝（申请等）
2. exclusive 专门的，独家的
3. sales agent 销售代理商

7-10 寻找贸易伙伴

We are a Chinese computer firm specializing in human voice recognition. We plan to expand our business into your country and have been searching for a prospective local partner. Several people have mentioned your name as a good candidate.

Are you in a position to explore the possibility of working with us? If so, we would like to set up an initial meeting with you. We are enclosing some literature to introduce ourselves.

Please let us hear your reaction as soon as possible. Thank you.

Words and Expressions

1. specializing in 专门从事
2. human voice recognition 人类声音识别
3. prospective 潜在的
4. local partner 当地客户
5. candidate 候补人
6. explore the possibility 展示可能性
7. initial 最初的；第一次
8. literature 资料
9. reaction 反应，答复

7-11 建立业务关系(1)

We saw your fat-reducing tea at the International Exhibition of National Health Products held in Italy during October, and are keenly interested in this product.

With a view to building trade relations with you, we are writing to you and hope to receive your catalogues and price-lists for reference.

Words and Expressions

1. fat-reducing tea 减肥茶

2. keenly 强烈地
3. With a view to 为了，为的是；目的在于
4. building trade relations 建立贸易关系

7-12　建立业务关系(2)

As one of the leading American importers of health products, we are experiencing in pushing sales of the products and have good connections with wholesalers and retailers in the country. If your prices are in line, we trust important business can materialize.

Words and Expressions

1. pushing sales 推销
2. good connections with 良好的人际关系
3. wholesalers and retailers 批发商和零售商
4. in line 一致，适当，有秩序
5. materialize 具体化，实质化；实现

7-13　建立业务关系(3)

We learned from the internet that you are in the market for jogging shoes with EVA sole, which just falls into our business scope. Our corporation, as a state-owned foreign trade organization, deals in the import and export of raw materials and relevant products for chemical industry.

We are writing to enter into business relations with you on a basis of mutual benefits and common developments.

Words and Expressions

1. jogging 慢跑，小跑
2. sole 鞋底
3. scope 范围
4. fall into our business scope 在我们的经营范围内
5. state-owned 国营的
6. relevant 相关的
7. mutual benefits 双边利益

7-14　建立业务关系(4)

We are interested in Chinese black tea which is fine in quality and low in price.

Being one of the largest importers of Chinese black tea in England, we shall be pleased to establish business relations with you.

It will be highly appreciated if you could send us some brochures and samples for our reference.

Words and Expressions

1. black tea 红茶
2. fine in quality and low in price 物美价廉
3. establish 建立

小知识　　　　　　　　国际贸易潜规则

商务交往中不得涉及的话题：
1. 非议国家和政府；
2. 国家和行业秘密；
3. 对方内部的事情；
4. 在背后议论领导、同事，说同行的坏话；
5. 格调不高的问题；
6. 私人问题五不问：不问收入；不问年龄；不问婚姻家庭；不问健康问题；不问经历。

7-15 回复建立业务关系

Thank you for your letter of January 10, 2019 and shall be glad to enter into business relations with your firm. Hope we have a good start on a basis of mutual benefits and common developments between the two countries.

Words and Expressions

1. enter into 开始；建立
2. basis of mutual benefits 互利互惠的基础上
3. common developments 共同发展

7-16 介绍公司业务

We have a Rubber Products Department in our factory, which specializes in the export of various kinds of shoes made in China including jogging shoes with EVA sole of fashionable designs, comfortable feeling, and high popularity in America, Europe and Asia.

Enclosed is our latest catalogue on jogging shoes with EVA sole, which may meet with your demand. If there isn't, please let us know your specific requirements.

Words and Expressions

1. various 各种各样的
2. fashionable designs 流行的设计
3. comfortable feeling 舒适的感觉
4. high popularity 知名度高
5. demand 需求
6. specific requirements 特殊要求

Exercise

Ⅰ. Fill in the blanks with the following words.

| export | quality | advantage | position | expand |
| mutual | establish | urge | needs | candidate |

1. We plan to _____ our business into your country and have been searching for a prospective local partner.
2. Several people have mentioned your name as a good _____ .
3. Are you in a _____ to explore the possibility of working with us?
4. We believe that this product will meet the _____ and tastes of individuals interested in healthy living.
5. You can take _____ of a special introductory sales price through October 31, 2019.
6. We _____ you not to pass up this opportunity.
7. We are interested in Chinese black tea which in fine _____ and low in price.
8. Being one of the largest importers of Chinese black tea in England, we shall be pleased to _____ business relations with you.
9. We deals in the import and _____ of raw materials and relevant products for chemical industry.
10. We are writing to enter into business relations with you on a basis of _____ benefits and common developments.

Ⅱ. Translate the following words and phrases.

Section A: Translate into English.

1. 贸易伙伴
2. 代理产品

3. 建立业务关系

4. 互利互惠

5. 扩大业务

Section B：Translate into Chinese.

1. wholesalers and retailers

2. a prospective customer

3. fashionable designs

4. common developments

5. Products Department

Ⅲ. Writing in English.

请给你的海外客户写一建立业务关系的信函。

8 Placing Orders
下订单

Aims to Obtain

Upon completion of the unit, you should：

- know how to write letters about placing an order；
- be able to make good use of the words or expressions to write the terms of payment, delievery, etc. before order；
- grasp some basic tactics about writing how to deal with kinds of problems about order.

8-1 随寄支票下单

Please send me five cases of 1988 Vintage Chardonnay as shown in your promotional catalog. I am enclosing a cashier's check for ＄896.00 to cover the cost of the merchandise and freight.

Prompt shipment will be appreciated.

Words and Expressions

1. 1988 Vintage Chardonnay

1988年的陈年夏敦埃酒（一种类似夏布利酒的无甜味白葡萄酒）

2. promotional catalog 促销目录

3. a cashier's check 银行开出的现金支票
4. cover the cost 支付成本费
5. freight 运费
6. prompt shipment 即期装运

8-2 发送订货单

In reference to your quotations of July 16, 2018, we are happy to place an order with you under our purchase order #MO776.

Please send your acceptance of our order together with a delivery schedule.

Words and Expressions

1. In reference to 关于
2. place an order 定购；预订
3. purchase order 购买单，定单
4. acceptance 接受；接纳
5. delivery schedule 交货计划

8-3 能马上交货作为前提条件的下订单

We would like to place the following order with you, provided you can guarantee prompt delivery.

50 Persian carpets: Model 30X50AS

The shipment must reach Kobe Port before June 5, 2019.

Please confirm your acceptance of our order and send us your invoice. Upon receipt of same, we will forward a bank draft to you. Thank you.

Words and Expressions

1. guarantee 保证；担保
2. prompt delivery 限时专送
3. Persian carpets 波斯地毯
4. Kobe Port 日本神户港
5. invoice 发票；开发票
6. Upon receipt of 一旦收到
7. a bank draft 银行汇票

8-4 取消订单

Just two weeks ago, I placed an order for an Osborn teacup set as per the enclosed copy of the order sheet. However, I regret that I must cancel that order.

Please accept this cancellation, and refund my payment at your earliest convenience. If my order has already been shipped, I will send it back to you upon receipt.

Thank you for your prompt action.

Words and Expressions

1. Osborn teacup set 德国奥斯本茶杯套
2. as per 根据……
3. order sheet 订货单
4. cancel 取消
5. accept this cancellation 接受取消
6. refund my payment 退款

8-5 订单内容变更

We recently placed an order for free-standing fireplaces on purchase order ♯MK600. However, we must make the following change in our order:

From: 28 units of model ♯4333

To: 20 units of model ♯4333, and 8 units of model ♯4334

Please advise if this is possible and if there will be any change in price. If necessary, send us a revised invoice.

As this change is very important to us, your cooperation will be much appreciated.

Words and Expressions

1. free-standing fireplaces 独立壁炉
2. revised 经过修订的
3. revised invoice 订正后的发票
4. purchase order 定单
5. advise 通知,告知

8-6 要求提前发货

In our letter of October 23, 2018, we ordered color pigment from your company. Delivery of this order is scheduled for December 5, 2018. However, we must now request an earlier shipment in order to meet an important customer's needs.

Please let us know if you can expedite delivery by the end of November.

Words and Expressions

1. pigment 颜料;给……着色;呈现颜色
2. expedite 加速进展

8-7 等待信用证的开设

Thank you for your recent order for our fish finders. This order has been processed for early shipment, pending your opening an irrevocable letter of credit in our favor for the minimum amount of $456,856, valid through April 30, 2019. Please advise your bank to appoint Bank of China, Beijing branch office as the receiving bank.

Once we confirm your L/C, we will notify you of the shipping schedule. Thank you.

Words and Expressions

1. fish finders 鱼群探测仪
2. process 处理;进行
3. pending 直到,等到,以……为条件
4. an irrevocable letter of credit 不可撤销的信用证
5. in our favor 以我方为受益人
6. minimum 最低限度
7. valid through 到……有效
8. appoint 约定,指定
9. notify 通知

8-8 初次订单要求发货前付款

We are pleased to have received your order for Yamato pearls. It is our corporate policy to ask the first-time buyer for pre-payment. Therefore, we will ship your order, as soon as we confirm your payment.

Thank you for your cooperation, and we hope this will be the beginning of a long-lasting business relationship.

Words and Expressions

1. corporate policy 公司的规定
2. first-time buyer 初购者
3. pre-payment 预付

4. ship your order 对你的订单商品发货

5. long-lasting 持久的；长期的

8-9 发货通知和付款资料的寄出通知

Please be advised that your order of fifty Yamaha jet skis left Dalian on OSK's vessel on march 30, 2019.

The shipping documents will be forwarded to your bank through the bank of China, Hangzhou branch, for-release against payment. Thank you for your business.

Words and Expressions

1. jet skis 水上摩托艇
2. OSK 日本大阪商船公司(Osaka Syosen Kaisha 的缩写)
3. vessel 船只
4. shipping documents 船运单据，(包含发票，装箱单，海运提单，保险单等单据)
5. be forwarded to 被转发给……
6. release against payment 付款后放行

8-10 最终确认订单商品

Thank you for your order ♯334455 for seals brand wet suits. Unfortunately, we are unable to process this order because your order identification numbers do not match ours.

Please refer to our catalog and indicate the catalog numbers. If you have any questions, call us at (306)3334-9987. As soon as we receive clarification of your order, we will process it for shipment. Thank you.

Words and Expressions

1. seals brand 海豹牌
2. wet suits 潜水衣；潜水服
3. identification number 识别数；标识号
4. match 一致
5. refer to 参考
6. indicate 表明；指示
7. clarification 澄清；明确，说明

小知识　　　　　　　　　　**OEM 产品**

OEM(Original Equipment Manufacturing)生产的产品，即代工生产，也称为贴

牌生产。基本含义为品牌生产者不直接生产产品，而是利用自己掌握的核心技术负责设计和开发新产品，控制销售渠道，具体的加工任务是按设计好的或确认的商品图样、规格、零件、半成品或成品，以及国外委托方规定的加工程序、方法和质量标准，通过合同订购的方式委托同类产品的其他厂家生产。之后将所订产品低价买断，并直接贴上自己的品牌商标，在国际市场上销售。

这种委托他人生产的合作方式简称OEM，承接加工任务的制造商生产的产品被称为OEM产品。可见，OEM生产属于加工贸易中的"代工生产"方式，在国际贸易中是以商品为载体的劳务出口。

例如，在中国众所周知的玩具猫Hello Kitty和休闲服装的优衣库是日本的品牌，日本人设计在中国广州、深圳等地的工厂生产的贴牌产品。日本及欧美市场上销售的Kitty Cat和优衣库全是中国制造。这就是典型的OEM产品。

8-11 要求按照新价格表下单

We received your order dated July 14, 2019. However, we are unable to accept your order at this time because it is based upon our old price schedule.

We are enclosing our current catalog and price list for your reference. Please re-submit the order, and we will be happy to process it promptly. Thank you very much.

Words and Expressions

1. accept your order 接受你们的订单
2. based upon 基于……
3. re-submit 重新提交
4. promptly 尽快，立刻

8-12 订单转交代理店的通知

Thank you for your order for Tanaka power tools. Since all sales of our products in India are handled by our sales agent, TDK Trading, your order has been transferred to them and they will be contacting you soon.

In the future, please direct your correspondence to:
Goto trading co.Ltd.
1-1-1 Sakae-machi, 3-chomre
Minato-ku, Tokyo 143-0000
Tel: (03)3455-6656
Fax: (03)3455-7890
E-mail: sales@gotot.cojp

Thank you again for your business.

> **Words and Expressions**

1. power tools 电动工具
2. handle 处理；操作
3. sales agent 销售代理商
4. be transferred to 被转交到……
5. correspondence 通信，信件
6. direct your correspondence to 直接把邮件寄给……

8-13 不能马上交货，用替代品的交货蹉商

In response to your request for immediate delivery of IC-20987, we regret to inform you that it will take us at least six weeks to arrange this shipment. However, we do have a similar model #IC-30060 in stock for immediate shipment at the same price.

Please let us know if this is an acceptable substitution. Thank you.

> **Words and Expressions**

1. In response to 对……做出回应
2. similar model 相似的型号
3. immediate shipment 立即发货
4. arrange 安排
5. in stock 有现货，有库存
6. acceptable substitution 可接受的替代品

8-14 因生产终止而拒绝的订单

We received your order for ZINK Brand alligator skin handbags. We are sorry we cannot accept the order, as this product line has been discontinued.

However, we have recently added several new items to our merchandise list. For your future reference, we are enclosing our current brochure. We hope we can be of service to you in the future.

> **Words and Expressions**

1. alligator skin 鳄鱼皮
2. this product line has been discontinued 这条生产线已经停产
3. items 商品，产品
4. merchandise list 商品单，商品表

8-15 因没付订金而导致的订单取消

We are sorry to advise you that we are unable to fill your order for 200 Banzai Brand automatic garage door openers. This unfortunate cancellation is the result of your failure to pay a down payment.

We regret taking this action, but we feel that we made it perfectly clear that prepayment was absolutely necessary. Of course, we will be happy to receive your re-order, together with a down payment.

Words and Expressions

1. fill 执行,履行
2. automatic 自动的
3. garage 车库
4. pay a down payment 付订金
5. prepayment 先付,预缴
6. absolutely 绝对地;完全地
7. re-order 重新订货;再订购

8-16 对订单的催货

We are very anxious to know about the shipment of our Order No. 322. We sent you 10 days ago an irrevocable letter of credit—expiration date being January 10, 2019.

As the season is approaching, our buyers are in urgent need of the goods. The contracted time of delivery rapidly falling due, it is imperative that you inform us the delivery time and effect shipment as soon as possible in order to enable the goods to arrive here in time to meet the demand of the selling season.

Your immediate effectuation of the shipment will be most appreciated.

Words and Expressions

1. be very anxious to 急切希望……
2. expiration date 截止日期;有效期
3. urgent need 急用
4. due 到期
5. imperative 必要的;不可避免的
6. selling season 销售旺季
7. effectuation 实行;完成

8-17 收到订单后的回复

Thank you for your inquiry of June 30. We're grateful to know that you are interested in our jet printers.

We enclose our latest price list together with a copy of our catalog. We're glad to tell you that we are always ready to provide you with good service. If you place regular orders for large quantities, we can offer you special discount.

We are looking forward to your first order.

Words and Expressions

1. grateful 感谢的；令人愉快的
2. jet printers 喷墨打印机
3. regular orders 定期订单
4. special discount 特别折扣

Exercise

Ⅰ. **Fill in the blanks with the following words.**

brochure	stock	clarification	refund	order
line	acceptable	least	cancel	indicate

1. Just two weeks ago, I placed an _____ for an Osborn teacup set as per the enclosed copy of the order sheet.
2. However, I regret that I must _____ that order.
3. Please accept this cancellation, and _____ my payment at your earliest convenience.
4. Please refer to our catalog and _____ the catalog numbers.
5. As soon as we receive _____ of your order, we will process it for shipment.
6. We regret to inform you that it will take us at _____ six weeks to arrange this shipment.
7. We do have a similar model ♯IC-30060 in _____ for immediate shipment at the price.
8. Please let us know if this is an _____ substitution.
9. For your future reference, we are enclosing our current _____ .
10. We are sorry we cannot accept the order, as this product _____ has been discontinued.

Ⅱ. Translate the following words and phrases.

Section A：Translate into English.

1. 取消订单

2. 提前付款

3. 发货时间

4. 替代品

5. 急需商品

Section B：Translate into Chinese.

1. confirm your payment

2. current catalog and price list

3. immediate shipment

4. correspondence

5. re-submit the order

Ⅲ. Writing in English.

请给你的海外客户写一封订单内容变更的信函。

9　Payment
付　款

Aims to Obtain

Upon completion of the unit，you should：

- know how to write letters about processing payment；
- be able to make good use of the words or expressions to write opening L/C, amending L/C and extending the expiration of L/C；
- grasp some basic tactics about writing the request of payment overdue.

9－1　要求信用证付款

Thank you for your order for 3000 tons of ♯50 steel rods. Your order is being processed to ensure early delivery.

In accordance with our agreement，please advise us when you have opened a letter of credit in our favor in the amount of ＄409,899, valid through September 30, 2019. Our receiving bank is Bank of China，Shanghai Branch.

Thank you again for your business.

85

Words and Expressions

1. steel rods 钢管
2. ensure 确保
3. in accordance with 按照
4. agreement 协议,合同书
5. in our favor 以我方为受益人
6. amount 金额,总额
7. valid 有效的

小知识　　　　　　　L/C(Letter of Credit)

L/C(Letter of Credit)即信用证,是进口人所在地的一家银行,应进口人的请求,向出口人开立的、有条件的保证付款的凭证。开证银行负首要付款责任。国际贸易中用得最多的一种付款方式。信用证在实际运用中有两大作用:

(1) 保证作用。采用信用证方式,只要出口人按信用证的要求提交单据,银行即保证付款,所以,它使出口商收款有保障。

(2) 资金负担较平衡。信用证支付方式对买方、卖方和银行的风险都相对较小,因而有利于国际贸易的顺利进行。

一流银行的L/C是卖方最认可的支付方式。中石化和俄罗斯的石油添加剂贸易中,俄罗斯要求中石化用L/C信用证方式支付,中石化按要求开了中国银行的L/C,但是被俄罗斯拒绝了。原因是在俄罗斯看来中国银行不是First Class Bank(一流银行),中方在明白这个潜规则后,想方设法开到了HSBC(英国汇丰银行)的L/C,才得以促使这笔贸易的成功。

9-2 信用证的开设通知

In reference to our order for wicker furniture, please be advised that we have instructed the Bank of Hong Kong to open a letter of credit for $300,590, valid until November 30, 2019. This credit will be confirmed by the Manhattan Bank in New York, which will accept your draft at thirty days after sight for the amount of your invoice.

Please inform us of your shipping schedule.

Words and Expressions

1. wicker furniture 柳条编制的家具
2. instruct 通知,要求
3. draft 汇票

4. after sight 见票后（指国际结算中的远期付款）

> 小知识　　　　　　　　　　**Manhattan（曼哈顿）**

曼哈顿是美国纽约市中心区，被形容为整个美国的经济和文化中心，是纽约市中央商务区所在地，世界上摩天大楼最集中的地区，汇集了世界500强中绝大部分公司的总部，也是联合国总部的所在地。曼哈顿的华尔街是世界上最重要的金融中心，有纽约证券交易所和纳斯达克，曼哈顿的房地产市场也是全世界最昂贵之一。

9-3 申请信用证期限延期和修改

Regarding your order for sheet metal galvanizing equipment, we regret to inform you that, due to unforeseen circumstances, there will be some delay in the delivery.

To accommodate this change, please amend the L/C by extending the expiration date from September 30, 2019 to November 30, 2019.

We are sorry for any inconvenience this may cause you and appreciate your cooperation.

Words and Expressions

1. metal galvanizing equipment 金属镀锌设备
2. unforeseen 意外的，无法预料的
3. circumstances 情况，状况（尤指经济状况）
4. delay 延迟；拖延；耽搁
5. accommodate this change 应对这个变化
6. amend 改良；修改
7. extending the expiration date 延长有效期

9-4 要求提供付款用的详细发票

We have received your invoice #21212 dated April 30, 2019, for your corporate tax return preparation service. The invoice shows only the total of $8,560 for your services. However, we require an itemized invoice detailing the charges for your services.

Once we receive such an invoice, we will be able to forward payment.

Words and Expressions

1. corporate tax return preparation service 企业纳税申报准备服务（业务）
2. itemized 分项扣除

3. detailing the charges for your services 细化服务费

9-5 电信付款(T/T)的通知

This is to notify you that payment of invoice ♯34567 has been executed this day, August 5, 2019. The amount of ＄67,900,00 has been wired to your account ♯006789 at Northwest Federal Bank, Portland, Oregon.

Please contact me if you experience any problem with this transfer.

Words and Expressions

1. execute 执行，完成；履行
2. wire to your account 电汇到你的账户
3. Northwest Federal Bank, Portland, Oregon 西北联邦银行，波特兰市，俄勒冈州(美国)
4. experience any problem 遇到任何问题
5. transfer 汇款

小知识   T/T

T/T(电汇)，是 Telegraphic Transfer 的缩写，指汇出行应汇款人申请，拍发加押电报/电传或 SWIFT 给在另一国家的分行或代理行(即汇入行)指示解付一定金额给收款人的一种汇款方式。电汇的特点是速度快、收费高，在国际贸易实际结算业务中运用最多。

另外还有两种汇款方式：M/T 信汇(Mail Transfer)，信汇的特点是费用较低，但收到汇款的时间较迟；D/D 票汇(Remittance by Bank is Demand Draft)，银行即期汇票。

9-6 遗失汇票的付款终止

Please be advised that we have instructed our bank to stop payment on check ♯30076 in the amount of ＄4,579,98 which you claim never arrived.

We are enclosing a replacement check, ♯30113 in the same amount. If our first check ever turns up, please void and return it to us. We are sorry for the inconvenience you have been caused by this incident.

Words and Expressions

1. instruct our bank to stop payment 指示银行停止付款
2. claim 声称；断言
3. replacement check 更换后的支票
4. amount 数量

5. turn up 出现

6. void 无效

7. inconvenience 不便

8. incident 事件；小插曲

9-7 催账信(温柔的语气)

It is noted that as of March 15, 2019, we have not received your payment for our invoice ♯50221 dated January $31, 2019. Please check your records and remit the payment immediately.

Perhaps your payment and our letter have crossed in the mail. If that is the case, please disregard this notice and accept our thanks.

Words and Expressions

1. as of March 15 到 3 月 15 日为止
2. check your records 检查你的记录
3. remit 汇款
4. cross in the mail 还在邮寄中
5. disregard this notice 无视这一通知

9-8 催账信(一般语气)

Your payment for $34,500, for our invoice ♯50668, dated March 15, 2019, has not been received at this writing. This payment is now three months overdue.

Please execute and remit this payment immediately. If there is any reason why payment cannot be made promptly, we would like to know it. Otherwise, we will expect the payment shortly. Thank you.

Words and Expressions

1. overdue 逾期的
2. execute and remit this payment 执行并汇款
3. otherwise 否则，不然

9-9 催账信(重语气)

Your payment of $34,500, against our invoice ♯50688, is now over three months in arrears. Also, you have ignored our repeated attempts to correspond with you regarding your account.

We believe you are aware of the seriousness of placing your previously good credit rating in jeopardy. If we do not receive your payment by 5:00 p.m. On June 25, 2019, we will have no alternative but to turn your case over to our collection agency. Thank you for your cooperation.

Words and Expressions

1. in arrears 拖欠(付款等)
2. ignore our repeated attempts 无视我们的再三催促
3. be aware of 意识到，注意到
4. seriousness 严重性
5. previously good credit rating 以前良好的信用评级
6. in jeopardy 处于危险状态
7. alternative 替代的；另类的；备选的；其他的
8. have no alternative but to 只得；不得已；别无选择
9. turn your case over to 把你的案子移交给……
10. collection agency 代收欠款的公司

9-10 催账信(最终通告)

Please be advised that our invoice #23456 is now 60 days overdue, we request immediate payment of the balance in full. Further delay may result in serious damage to your credit rating and to our business relationship.

Thank you for your prompt attention to this matter.

Words and Expressions

1. 60 days overdue 已经拖欠60天
2. balance 余额
3. further delay 进一步的延迟
4. serious damage 严重损害
5. credit rating 信用等级

9-11 收到催账信后的道歉

Thank you for your letter regarding the balance owed against your invoice #50221. We have checked our records and found, with much embarrassment, that due to our oversight, the invoice had not been paid.

We immediately processed payment. You may expect the money within five working days. Please accept our apology for this delay.

Words and Expressions

1. owed 欠……债，应该支付的
2. with much embarrassment 极为尴尬
3. oversight 疏忽
4. process 处理，进行操作
5. within five working days 在五个工作日内
6. apology 道歉

9-12　收到催账信后要求延期支付

We received your notice concerning our overdue payment of ＄300,150. Due to unforeseen circumstances, we will be unable to pay until December 1, 2019.

Your understanding and patience with us will be greatly appreciated. Needless to say, we will pay sooner if at all possible. Thank you for your cooperation.

Words and Expressions

1. unforeseen 不可预测的
2. due to unforeseen circumstances 由于无法预料的经济状况
3. needless to say 不必说；当然

9-13　收到催账信后的支付

We received your collection notice dated May 2, 2019. According to our records, we sent you a check on April 1, 2019, for the entire balance of ＄57,900.

Please examine your records, and let us know if you received this payment.

Words and Expressions

1. collection notice 托收通知书
2. entire 整体的
3. examine your records 检查你们的记录

9-14　为了按时发货要求信用证有效期延长

We acknowledge the receipt of your L/C No. 518 issued by the Commercial Bank of Shenzhen covering the order No. 625. As stipulated in the relevant contract, shipment should be made not later than December 25, 2019. However, we received your L/C only yesterday and it is impossible for us to ship the goods on time.

Under the circumstances, we regret to have to request you to extend the above

L/C to January 15, 2019 and January 5, 2019 for shipment.

Please see to it that your amendment reach us by December 30, 2019, otherwise shipment will be further delayed.

Words and Expressions

1. acknowledge 告知已收到
2. issue 发行
3. Commercial Bank of Shenzhen 深圳商业银行
4. stipulate (尤指在协议或合同中的)规定,约定
5. As stipulated in the relevant contract 按照有关合同的规定
6. under the circumstances 在这种情况下
7. amendment 修改;修订

9-15 托收条款

After shipment, the seller shall send through the seller's bank a draft drawn on the buyer together with the shipping documents to the buyer through the buyer's bank for collection.

Words and Expressions

1. draft 汇票
2. a draft drawn on the buyer 买方开出的汇票
3. collection 托收

小知识　　　　　　　　collection 托收

托收是国际贸易中的一种付款方式。是指出口人出具债权凭证(汇票等)委托银行向进口人收取货款的一种支付方式。也就是通常说的货到付款。这种支付方式也存在风险。如果买家收到商品后逃之夭夭,卖方收不到货款对卖方来说也是损失。特别是在欧洲金融危机期间,据英国外贸企业说很多 bad customer(指的是进了货而没付款的不太好的客户),因此这些英国外贸企业不愿意先发货,不喜欢采用这种的国际结算方式。

9-16 要求电信汇款

The buyers shall pay the total value to the sellers in advance by T/T no later than this Friday.

As soon as we see the money in our account, we will send the bags by TNT immediately.

Words and Expressions

1. total value 总货款
2. in advance 预先,提前
3. no later than 不晚于,不迟于
4. account 账户
5. TNT 荷兰天地(荷兰快递运输公司)

小知识　　　　　　　　TNT

TNT 快递为企业和个人提供快递和邮政服务。均为航空急件传递方式(air express service)

TNT 快递成立于 1946 年,总部位于荷兰的 TNT 集团,提供世界范围内的包裹、文件以及货运项目的安全准时运送服务。特别在欧洲和亚洲可提供高效的递送网络,早在 1988 年,TNT 就已进入中国市场。目前,TNT 为客户提供从定时的门到门快递服务和供应链管理,到直邮服务的整合业务解决方案。TNT 在中国拥有 25 直属运营分支机构,3 个全功能国际口岸和近 3 000 名员工,服务范围覆盖中国 500 多个城市。

迄今为止,在 200 多个国家和地区拥有网络并开展大规模业务的全球性快递公司还有以下 3 个;连同 TNT 被称为世界快递行业的 4 大航母

UPS　美国联合包裹运输

DHL　美国与德国合资的邮政集团品牌/德国敦豪

Fedex　美国联邦快递

9-17 收到付款

This is a confirmation regarding your payment of US $10,000. It has been cashed to our account.

Thank you for your cooperation on this transaction and we assure you always of our best and immediate service.

Words and Expressions

1. have been cashed to our account 已经兑现到我们的帐户
2. transaction 交易
3. assure 保证

9-18 公司财务报告

Director's Report

Date of Report: January 1, 2019

Dear Sir or Madam:

The Directors take pleasure in submitting their Report on Account with regard to the annual financial condition ended December 31, 2018.

During the year, in spite of the fact that we were faced with many difficulties and challenges, we were still able to maintain the steady increase in our profits. The following is the Account for the year under review:

Net Profit　　US $6,000,000

Amount Brought Forward from Last Year　　US $800,000

Total Profit　　US $6,800,000

Interim Divided　　US $100,000

Final Divided　　UU $200,000

Balance　　US $3,700,000

By Order of the Board of Directors

Michael Lee

signature: Michael Lee

Words and Expressions

1. annual financial condition 年度财务状况
2. in spite of 虽然,尽管……
3. steady 稳定的
4. maintain the steady increase 保持稳定的增长
5. net profit 纯利润
6. interim 中期
7. balance 余额
8. by order of 奉……之命
9. the Board of Directors 董事会

小知识　　USD(美元)的强势

世界上能够用什么货币买石油？英镑、欧元、澳币等发达国家的货币都不在此范围,唯有美利坚合众国的货币 USD(美元)才能买到。这是美国和 OPEC 世界石油输出组织的约定。美国不允许任何人改变这个约定也体现出了在国际贸易中用美元成交的垄断性,这也是美国成为世界经济总体第一的原因之一。

Exercise

Ⅰ. Fill in the blanks with the following words.

| pay | made | overdue | inconvenience | in |
| problem | notify | aware | delay | execute |

1. This is to _____ you that payment of invoice ♯34567 has been executed this day, August 5, 2001.
2. Please contact me if you experience any _____ with this transfer.
3. We are sorry for the _____ you have been caused by this incident.
4. Perhaps your payment and our letter have crossed _____ the mail.
5. This payment is now there months _____ .
6. Please _____ and remit this payment immediately.
7. If there is any reason why payment cannot be _____ promptly, we would like to know it.
8. Further _____ may result in serious damage to your credit rating and to our business relationship.
9. The buyers shall _____ the total value to the sellers in advance by T/T no later than this Friday.
10. We believe you are _____ of the seriousness of placing your previously good credit rating in jeopardy.

Ⅱ. Translate the following words and phrases.

Section A: Translate into English.
1. 账号
2. 开设信用证
3. 商业银行
4. 电信汇款
5. 托收

Section B: Translate into Chinese.
1. extending the expiration date
2. the relevant contract
3. financial condition
4. remit the payment
5. check your records

Ⅲ. **Writing in English.**

请给你的贸易伙伴写一封已经开设信用证的通知。

10　A Credit Reference
　　　信用查询

> **Aims to Obtain**
>
> **Upon completion of the unit, you should:**
> - know how to write letters about the request of a bank reference;
> - be able to make good use of the words or expressions to write application for credit reference and credit transactions, etc..

10-1　要求对新顾客进行信用调查

Thank you for your order for our water pumps. In as much as this is our first business transaction with you, we require the following:

—Your major banks and account numbers.

—Two business creditors as references.

Your order will be shipped upon receipt of the above information.

Words and Expressions

1. water pumps 水泵
2. in as much as 因为;由于
3. business transaction 商业交易;业务交易
4. account numbers 账号
5. as references 作为参考

10-2　请求银行信用调查

We are currently processing a credit application from Lock Corporation 123 Main Street, New York, who have given your name as a bank reference.

We would like to request a credit review from your bank. Please provide general information on the firm and its financial standing. We are particularly interested in knowing their average monthly balance.

Thank you in advance for your cooperation.

Words and Expressions

1. currently processing a credit application 目前正在处理信用申请
2. general information on the firm 公司概况
3. financial standing 财政状况
4. average 平均的
5. monthly balance 每月余额

10-3 向银行依赖推荐书

In our recent efforts to advance our market into South Africa, we need a strong reference from a banking institution.

We would appreciate it if you could write a favorable letter of reference with emphasis on our solid financial strength. The letter should be sent to us at your earliest convenience.

I will call you in a week or so as a follow-up to this request. Thank you for your assistance.

Words and Expressions

1. banking institution 金融机构
2. emphasis on 强调
3. solid financial strength 雄厚的资金实力
4. letter of reference 推荐书
5. follow-up 跟踪；随访；后续行动

10-4 良好的信用查询

We are happy to save as a credit reference for Syntax Corporation.

We have been conducting business with Syntax for the past five years, and this company has an outstanding credit record with us. We have no hesitation in encouraging a favorable decision.

Words and Expressions

1. conduct business with 与……开展业务
2. an outstanding credit record 优秀的信用记录
3. have no hesitation 毫不犹豫
4. favorable 赞同的

10-5 拒绝对交易伙伴的信用查询

We have received your request concerning a credit reference for Jasper Services. At this time, we regret that we cannot offer such a reference since we are no longer doing business with the company.

We are sorry that we are unable to help you.

Words and Expressions

1. concerning 关于
2. a credit reference 信用调查
3. no longer 不再

10-6 承诺信用交易申请

Thank you for your recent application for credit at Nitto Jimukiki Co, Ltd.. We are pleased to inform you that your company's application has been approved to a maximum credit level of $30,000.

Statements are sent on a monthly basis and payments are due upon receipt. We look forward to serving you.

Words and Expressions

1. maximum credit level of $30,000 最大信用额度达到3万美元
2. statement 结算单
3. on a monthly 按月
4. be due upon receipt 一旦收到必须支付

10-7 拒绝信用交易申请

We regret to inform you that your application for credit transactions at Nike Sports Supplies has not been approved at this time due to your failure to provide the requested references.

We will be happy to review your credit rating in the future. Until then, we will continue to serve you on a cash basis.

Words and Expressions

1. inform 通知
2. application for credit transactions 信用交易申请书
3. approve 批准

4. due to 由于；因为

5. credit rating 资信评级，信用评级

6. until then 直到那时

Exercise

Ⅰ. Fill in the blanks with the following words.

| payments | financial | serve | balance | credit |

1. We would like to request a _____ review from your bank.
2. Please provide general information on the firm and its _____ standing.
3. We are particularly interested in knowing their average monthly _____.
4. Statements are sent on a monthly basis and _____ are due upon receipt.
5. Until then, we will continue to _____ you on a cash basis.

Ⅱ. Translate the following words and phrases.

Section A：Translate into English.

1. 信用调查
2. 财务报告
3. 业务交易

Section B：Translate into Chinese.

1. a bank reference
2. financial standing
3. an outstanding credit record

11　Job Search
　　求　职

Aims to Obtain

Upon completion of the unit, you should：

- know how to write letters about personal resume;
- be able to make good use of the words or expressions to write application for position;
- grasp some basic tactics about writing the result of interviewing.

11-1 应聘(1)

I am very interested in your recent ad in the *New York Times* for the position of office manager.

As my enclosed resume shows, I have the skills and experience to meet the qualifications. My major strength is patience with customers. I will be happy to supply reference upon request.

I would welcome the opportunity meet with you in person.

Words and Expressions

1. ad 广告(advertisement 的缩写)
2. major strength 主要长处,优点
3. patience with customers 耐心待客
4. qualifications 资格;资质
5. meet with you in person 亲自,直接与你面谈

11-2 应聘(2)

I'm writing to apply for the post of secretary to General Manager in your company.

As you will see from the enclosed C.V., I am 24 years old. I graduated from Heilongjiang Technical College in 2019. I majored in Business Administration. I had received very good grades in each course. In addition, I also have received the training of shorthand and typing. I am able to take shorthand at 90 words per minute and type 70 words a minute.

I have two years' experience in Business Administration and am looking for greater challenges and increased responsibility.

I would be very grateful for the opportunity to meet and could be available at any time for an interview.

Words and Expressions

1. apply for the post of 申请……职位
2. secretary to General Manager 总经理秘书
3. administration 管理
4. in addition 此外
5. shorthand and typing 速记和打字

11-3 积极的推销自己

Are you in need of capable multi-lingual receptionist in your company? If so, please consider me as candidate for the position. I have strong language skills in English, Spanish and French, as you can see from my enclosed resume. I can also provide excellent references at your request.

I would welcome an early opportunity to meet with you. Thank you.

Words and Expressions

1. in need of 需要
2. capable 能干的,有能力的
3. multi-lingual 多语言的
4. receptionist 接待员
5. candidate 候选人

11-4 对求职者的面试通知

After reviewing your resume, we feel you have qualification for the position of sales manager. We would like to interview you on October 31, 2019, at 1:00 p.m., at UMC Administration Office, 1234 Madison Ave., New York.

Please call David Chen at (212)337-0078 as soon as possible to let us know if you have received this notification. We look forward to meeting you.

Words and Expressions

1. review 阅读,审查
2. qualification 资格,资质
3. Ave. 大街,大道(Avenue 的缩写)
4. Administration Office 管理部
5. notification 通知;通知单

小知识　　　　　　　　　　UMC

UMC(United Microelectronics Corporation),台湾联华电子公司,是世界著名的半导体承包制造商。美国纽约证券交易所代号:UMC,台湾证券交易所代号:2303。该公司利用先进的工艺技术专为主要的半导体应用方案生产各种集成电路(IC)。联华电子在台湾、日本、新加坡、欧洲及美国均设有办事处,在全球各地的员工共计 13,000 多名。

11-5 录取通知

We are happy to offer you the position of financial analyst, effective September 1, 2019. Congratulations!

Please call 03-3334-5565 immediately to arrange a meeting with Mr. Smith to review the employment agreement. We look forward to working with you.

Words and Expressions

1. offer the position 提供职位
2. financial analyst 财务分析师
3. effective September 1, 2019 从2019年9月1日开始有效
4. employment agreement 就业协议

11-6 不录取通知

Thank you for your application for the position of intern. While we are impressed with your strong academic background, we regret that the position has already been filled. We will, however, keep your resume on file for possible future consideration. Thank you.

TELEDYNE JAPAN K.K.
AN ALLEGHENY TELEDYNE COMPANY
1-3-2 Iidabashi, Chiyoda-ku, Tokyo 102-0072
TEL: (3) 3239-9080 FAX: (3) 3239-9021

May 26, 2019

Dear Ms. Sou Kou,

Thank you for your application with curriculum vitae addressed to our company.

We have carefully reviewed your application and background information, however, we are sorry that at present we have no vacancy available for you.

Thank you for your interest in our company. We wish you success in finding your position in the near future.

Sincerely yours,
Teledyne Japan K.K.

Hajime Murase
Controller

Words and Expressions

1. intern 实习生
2. academic background 学术背景
3. fill 填充,充满
4. file 文件

11-7 退休后的再求职

As a recently retired computer engineer, I am very interested in volunteering my time for young people. Do you need my service in your school? I am available on an ongoing basis two or three days a week, and would be pleased to have an opportunity to work with the students.

Thank you very much, and I look forward to hearing from you.

Words and Expressions

1. retired 退休的
2. volunteering my time for young people 腾出时间志愿为年轻人做奉献
3. ongoing 不间断的;进行的

11-8 求职简历

Resume

Personal Data:

Name: Jiang Xiaoyan

Sex: Female

Date of Birth: May 15, 1992

Nationality: the Han

Marital Status: Single

Health: Excellent, no physical limitation

Marital Status: 66.Jingyu Ave.Yubei District,

Chongqing, 400078

Telephone Number: 023-63578218

Mobile Phone: 13997018245   Wechat: xy6453219

E-mail: 5789632@qq.com

Job Objective:

To obtain a position as a sales manager

Educational Background:

Sept. 2014 to June 2017: the degree of Master of Economics, Beijing University

Sept. 2010 to June 2014: the degree of Bachelor of Economics, Chongqing University

English Proficiency:

CET-6, able to read, speak and translate English

Honors:

Winner of University Scholarship, 2011-2012

Excellent Student, 2013-2014

Hobbies:

Enjoy computer programming, outdoor sports

Words and Expressions

1. marital status 婚姻状况
2. physical limitation 身体方面的限制
3. English proficiency 英语水平
4. outdoor sports 野外活动
5. degree of Bachelor 学士学位
6. degree of Master 硕士学位
7. scholarship 奖学金

实用案例

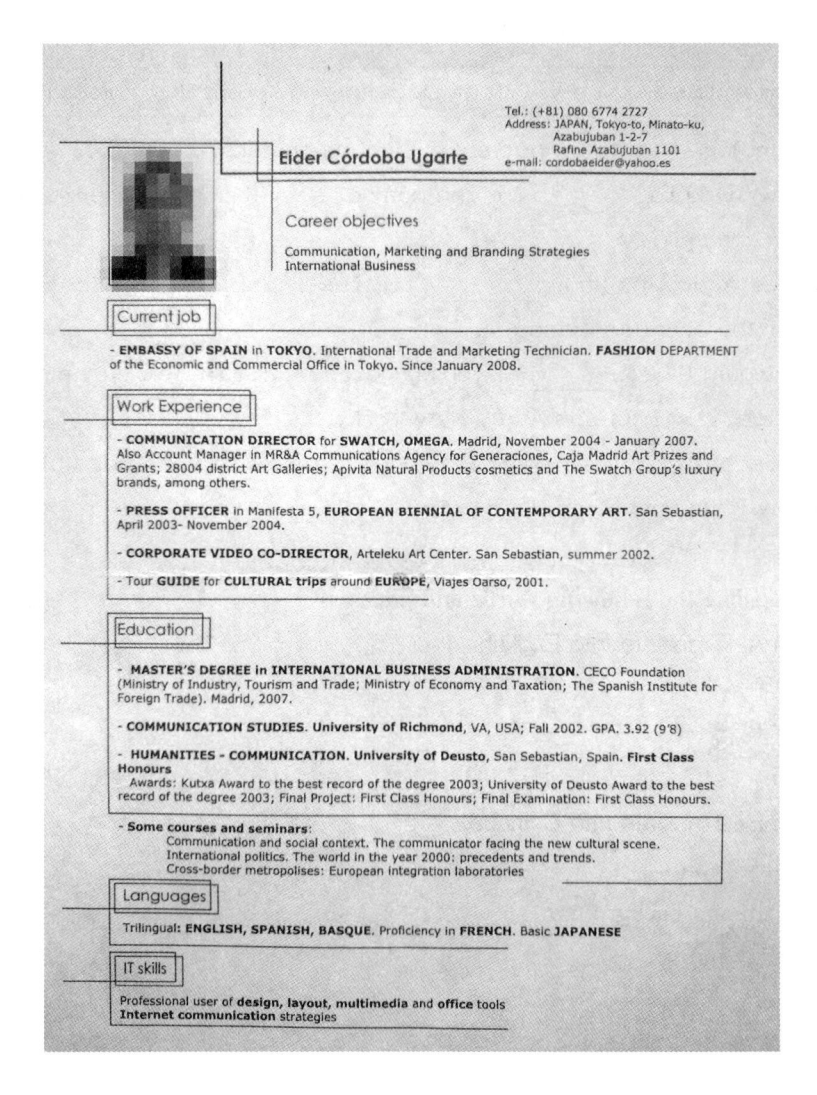

11-9 了解新工作近况

Just checking in with you to see how you're doing in your new job. I hope you like it and that it relates to what you have been studying. Pleases drop me a line and let me know about your new work and your family. Say "howdy" to your boyfriend for me.

Words and Expressions

1. check in with 检查，了解
2. relate to 涉及
3. drop me a line 写信给我
4. howdy 你好

Exercise

Ⅰ. Fill in the blanks with the following words.

| interview | apply | notification | strength | resume |

1. My major _____ is patience with customers.
2. I'm writing to _____ for the post of secretary to General Manager in your company.
3. After reviewing your _____, we feel you have qualification for the position of sales manager.
4. We would like to _____ you on October 31,2019, at 1:00 p.m., at UMC Office,1234 Madison Ave., New York.
5. Please call David Chen at (212)337-0078 as soon as possible to let us know if you have received this _____.

Ⅱ. Translate the following words and phrases.

Section A：Translate into English.
1. 面试
2. 语言技能
3. 简历

Section B：Translate into Chinese.
1. qualification
2. educational background
3. marital status

Ⅲ. Writing in English.

请给一家贸易公司写一封求职简历。

12 Product Consultation
咨　询

Aims to Obtain

Upon completion of the unit, you should：

• know how to write letters about various inquiries;

- be able to make good use of the words or expressions to write applying catalog, sample, price information, etc.;
- grasp some basic tactics about writing the request for the exhibition.

12-1 请求发送意向商品资料

Your recent ad in *ASIAN MARKET* caught our attention. We are very interested in learning more about your products. Please send us information on the latest models.

Thank you for your prompt reply.

Words and Expressions

1. catch our attention 引起我们的注意
2. latest 最新的
3. prompt 立刻的
4. *ASIAN MARKET*《亚洲市场》杂志名

12-2 请求发送商品邮购目录

I have heard about your catalog sales program, and l am very interested in knowing more about your merchandise.

Do you retail your merchandise directly to China? If so, please send me a copy of your current catalog together with information on payment, shipping charges, insurance, and delivery time.

If you charge for the catalog, please send a bill with the catalog. I am looking forward to hearing from you soon. Thank you.

Words and Expressions

1. retail 零售
2. shipping charges 运输费
3. insurance 保险
4. merchandise 商品
5. delivery time 交货时间
6. bill 账单

12-3　寄送客户要求的资料

Thank you for your letter of March 12, 2019, indicating an interest in our line of products. Therefore, we have enclosed a copy of our general catalog together with brochures of our products. If you need further information, please contact us. We will be happy to arrange for our representative to visit you.

Thank you again for your interest in our products.

Words and Expressions

1. line of product 产品范围
2. basic information 基本信息
3. general catalog 总商品目录
4. further 进一步的
5. representative 代表

12-4　申请商品样品

Having looked through your catalog, we are interested in marketing in China your Rainbow Sprinkler Heads.

Please send us, by airmail, one set of the merchandise as a sample of no value. We would be happy to pay the cost and airmail postage if necessary. Thank you for your prompt reply.

Words and Expressions

1. look through 仔细检查，详细阅读
2. sprinkler head 洒水头
3. a sample of no value 免费样品
4. airmail postage 航空邮费

12-5　回复样品申请

Thank you for your interest in our merchandise. As you requested, we have arranged to send a bag for your examination by air mail. You can expect delivery in a few days.

We hope that you will find the sample satisfactory to your need, and look forward to an opportunity to serve you in the near future.

Words and Expressions

1. merchandise 商品
2. arrange to 安排
3. delivery 发货
4. serve 服务；提供

12-6 有关产品进口的事宜

We have recently become acquainted with your free standing fireplace, and are interested in purchasing one of your latest models.

Do you ship merchandise to China? If so, please quote CIF Shanghai on all available models, indicating the normal delivery time and payment requirements. If you do not handle exporting, please advise whom we should contact for this service. Thank you for your prompt reply.

Words and Expressions

1. acquainted 了解；熟悉的
2. free standing fireplace 可自由设置位置的壁炉
3. latest models 最新的型号
4. CIF Shanghai 价格含成本加保险费加运费，运往上海（国际贸易术语 Cost, Insurance and Freight 的缩写）
5. purchasing 购买；采购
6. handle exporting 经营出口

小知识　　　　　　　　　　**国际贸易术语**

贸易术语又称贸易条件、价格术语（Price Terms），是一种"对外贸易的语言"（the Language of Foreign Trade）。具体是指用短语或英文缩写来说明买卖双方在交接货物过程中各自承担的义务和价格构成的专门用语。国际商会制定了13种贸易术语，并颁布了这些贸易术语作统一解释的《2010年国际贸易术语解释通则》，该通则已经成为全球贸易商遵循的国际规则。13种贸易术语如下：

- E 组：EXW
- F 组：FCA、FAS、FOB
- C 组：CFR、CIF、CPT、CIP
- D 组：DAF、DES、DEQ、DDU、DDP

12-7　投标申请与资料请求

We have recently learned from the media that you plan to purchase 30 coast patrol boats. We would like the opportunity to bid on this project.

Pan Pacific Motorboats is a reputable boat dealer with strong supply sources, and we are confident of our ability to offer the most attractive bid.

Please rush all the necessary information in an envelope addressed to me.

Words and Expressions

1. coast patrol boats 海岸巡逻艇
2. bid 投标；出价
3. dealer 经销商
4. supply sources 供应源
5. reputable 有信誉的；值得尊敬的
6. rush 赶快寄出

12-8　委托推荐代理店

We are an engineering firm specializing in telecommunications in China. Having established a successful business here, we are ready to expand our market into Mexico.

We are currently seeking recommendations for a reputable marketing company that could affiliate with us to do business in Mexico.

Enclosed is a copy of our company's profile. We would appreciate whatever assistance you can give us. Thank you.

Words and Expressions

1. specialize in 专门从事……
2. telecommunications 电信
3. seek 寻找；探寻
4. recommendation 推荐
5. affiliate with 使附属；加入，为……工作
6. profile 简介，概要

12-9　有关广告宣传费的事宜

We are a hi-tech company located in London, UK. We are interested in placing a display ad in your magazine.

Please send us your advertising rate sheet, as well as the cost of in-house artwork. Thank you for your prompt reply.

Words and Expressions

1. hi-tech 高科技
2. a display ad 大版面的广告(ad 是英文 advertisement 的缩写,即名词"广告"的意思,display 是"显示,大面积"的意思)
3. advertising rate sheet 广告费率表
4. in-house artwork 内部的艺术工作,指客户提供的宣传文以外广告公司内加工制作的图、表等艺术工作

12-10 有关客服的咨询事宜

I have recently learned that your association provides members with substantial discounts on first-class hotels throughout the nation.

I am interested in joining your association and would like to receive information about your services and benefits. Also, please send me a membership application. Thank you very much.

Words and Expressions

1. provide sb. with sth. 为谁提供……
2. substantial 大量的(反义词是 nominal)
3. first-class 一流的
4. throughout the nation 在全国各地
5. benefits 受益,恩惠
6. membership application 会员申请表

12-11 演讲邀请

The Beijing Pharmacologists Association regularly holds lecture meetings for its members to hear leaders and specialists in related industries.

I am writing to ask if you would kindly speak at our luncheon meeting on September 3, 2019, at the Hilton Hotel in Beijing. I will call you soon to discuss the details of the program.

We are hoping for a positive reply. Thank you very much.

Words and Expressions

1. pharmacologists 药理学家

2. association 协会

   3. regularly 定期的

   4. luncheon 午餐会

小知识　　　　　　　**Luncheon 与 Lunch 的区别**

　　如果是与他人共进的较正式的午餐会或午餐宴会，通常要用比较正式的 luncheon。例如，当今较流行的工作餐叫作 a business luncheon。人们可边吃边谈工作，同时又可促进友谊，可谓一举三得。此外，有时用于某种庆典之后举行的午餐会，也是用 luncheon 这个正式用词。

　　现代生活繁忙，许多人对于午餐都采取随便应付的态度。譬如，有的在办公室吃三明治(Sandwich)加一杯咖啡或奶茶，有的买点炸鸡腿和炸薯条(Fish and Chips)，还有的也许只来个巨无霸汉堡包(Hamburger)，或者吃些热狗(Hot Dog)就算了。这样的午餐因为量少且简单，只能算便餐(Light Lunch)。即便是稍丰盛一点的午餐，通常也只能称为 lunch。

12-12 拒绝演讲邀请

　　It is indeed a great honor for me to be invited as the keynote speaker at the Marine insures' Annual Convention in Hong Kong of kind of opportunity. Unfortunately, I cannot accept your invitation due to a prior commitment. However, I hope you will consider me at another time.

　　I wish you every success with the convention.

Words and Expressions

   1. indeed 的确；确实

   2. honor 光荣，荣幸

   3. keynote 基调；主旨

   4. the Marine insures' Annual Convention 海洋保险年会

   5. invitation 邀请

   6. prior commitment 优先承诺

12-13 请求撰写新闻稿

　　The October, 2019, edition of "Child Psychology" will feature a discussion on foreign language acquisition. We would like to ask you to contribute an article of about 5 000 words on the subject of "IQ and Foreign Language Learning Ability."

　　If you are unable to accommodate this request, please let us know. Otherwise, we look forward to receiving your manuscript on or before August 30, 2019. I will call you soon to discuss further details. Thank you very much.

Words and Expressions

1. Child Psychology 儿童心理学
2. feature a discussion 专题讨论
3. acquisition 获得；收获
4. accommodate this request 满足这一要求
5. IQ 智商，即智力商数(Intelligence Quotient)，系个人智力测验成绩和同年龄被试成绩相比的指数，是衡量个人智力高低的标准。智商概念是美国斯丹福大学心理学家特曼教授提出的。
6. otherwise 否则；另外
7. manuscript 手稿

12-14 再度确认

On March 12, 2019, I sent you a letter regarding my interest in M.B.A. program. Since I have not received a reply, perhaps my letter did not reach you. I am enclosing a copy of my previous letter, and hope to hear from you shortly.

Thank you for your attention.

Words and Expressions

1. M.B.A. Master of Business Administration 工商管理硕士
2. enclose 把……装入信封；附入
3. previous 先前的，前面的
4. shortly 不久；立刻；马上
5. attention 关注，关心

12-15 准备制作新商品册

Now we are on preparation of New System Leaflet. We will wait until I receive a feedback and decide then what to do. But please go ahead with the translation anyway. I will contact you as soon as I have any news regarding the system catalogue and when the files of the other leaflets will be uploaded.

I hope to solve this task to your complete satisfaction.

Words and Expressions

1. leaflet 商品册
2. feedback 反馈；反应

3. go ahead 前进；开始实施

4. uploaded 上传；上载

5. complete satisfaction 完全满意；称心如意

12-16 办展事宜咨询

In relation to the request for the exhibition of Mr. Akira Kai, please calculate all the expense and offer us the quotation so that we can make decision. If you can not organize this event, please ask some local company to make quotation for this purpose.

The concrete idea is follows:

1. place: Shanghai Art Museum or recommendable place.
2. exhibition period: one week in June.
3. seminar during exhibition: twice (about three hours once).
4. space: about 300 m^2 (about 60 works will be exhibited).

Waiting for your reply soon.

Words and Expressions

1. calculate 计算
2. expense 费用
3. quotation 报价表
4. concrete 具体的
5. recommendable place 值得推荐的地方
6. exhibition period 展期
7. seminar 研讨会
8. space 场地，空间

12-17 办展事宜咨询回复

For Mr. Liu Guoming's work exhibition, we contacted the Shanghai Art Museum and got below information.

1. They have hall available from June 20 - July 20 on third floor, size is 600 square meter. Price RMB 6,400 per day.

2. To organize an exhibition in all the Museum in Shanghai, they need the organizer to provide below information for approval.

—The introduction of organizer, it means Mr. Liu Guoming's need to provide his company details if he wants to use his company as organizer, or using personal entity Mr. Liu Guoming need to provide his own portfolio for inspection.

—Mr. Liu Guoming also need to prepare a letter to explain the purpose why he want to exhibit his job in the Museum.

——Mr. Liu Guoming also need to provide the file for the work he prepare to exhibit for the Museum to inspect and approve. This is a normal procedure to check all the exhibit works before they go to public.

If Mr. Liu Guoming think the date after June 20 is OK, can he arrange send us his company details or his personal portfolio together with the exhibit file. So that we can submit to the Museum for approval.

Words and Expressions

1. square meter 平方米
2. approval 批准
3. entity 实体；实际存在的
4. portfolio 代表作品
5. inspection 检查
6. normal procedure 正常办理手续，常规程序

12-18 咨询介绍客户事宜

It is our pleasure to communicate you with a good hope to realize business with you. One of our big customer's staff who is responsible for China is visiting Motor Show in Shanghai soon on 21 April. On this occasion we are advising him to visit you and see the studios in your company since they are one of a very good potential customers who use Broncolor and studios in Beijing and Shanghai. He is very much interested in the possibility of shooting picture in Shanghai as a photographer with your organization.

Please count this point and arrange your time for meeting with them in Shanghai at their hotel. We will inform you of the name of hotel they will stay.

Looking forward to hear from you soon.

Words and Expressions

1. realize 实现
2. be responsible for 负责，主管
3. Motor Show in Shanghai 上海车展
4. occasion 场合
5. potential 潜在的
6. Broncolor 布朗（品牌名，瑞士闪光灯摄影器材）
7. photographer 摄影师

12-19 快递费

We will send C200 flashtube to Shanghai Zenith today or tomorrow. The price should be the same as last time. How about EMS cost? Can we charge it to them?

Words and Expressions

1. flashtube 闪光灯
2. EMS 万国邮联（邮政快递）
3. charge 收费

12-20 咨询商品价格和售后服务

We are very much interested in the jet printers manufactured by your HP Company. We'd like to know your prices and after-sale services. If you send us your lowest quotations and provide good services, we would consider placing an order.

Looking forward to your prompt reply.

Words and Expressions

1. jet printer 喷墨打印机
2. manufacture 生产
3. quotations 报价
4. after-sale services 售后服务
5. placing an order 下订单
6. prompt 迅速的；立刻的

Exercise

Ⅰ. Fill in the blanks with the following words.

| feedback | purchase | quotation | ad | retail |
| ahead | bid | market | bill | complete |

1. Do you _____ your merchandise directly to China?
2. If you charge for the catalog, please send a _____ with the catalog.
3. Your recent _____ in "ASIAN MARKET" caught our attention.
4. I hope to solve this task to your _____ satisfaction.
5. If you can not organize this event please ask some local company to make _____ for this purpose.
6. Having established a successful business here, we are ready to expand our

_____ into Mexico.

7. We have recently learned from the media that you plan to _____ 30 coast patrol boats.

8. We would like the opportunity to _____ on this project.

9. We will wait until I receive a _____ and decide then what to do.

10. But please go _____ with the translation anyway.

Ⅱ. **Translate the following words and phrases.**

Section A：Translate into English.

1. 正常发货时间
2. EMS 快递费
3. 投标
4. 售后服务
5. 广告

Section B：Translate into Chinese.

1. prompt reply
2. the necessary information
3. seeking recommendations
4. expand our market
5. a successful business

Ⅲ. **Writing in English.**

请给你的海外制造商写一封申请商品样品的信函。

13 Claims and Settlement
争议与处理

Aims to Obtain

Upon completion of the unit, you should：

- know how to write letters about claim；
- be able to make good use of the words or expressions to ask changing defective merchandise, reissuing a corrected invoice, refund overpaid, etc.；
- grasp some basic tactics about writing the settlement of claim.

13-1　要求替换破损商品

I have received your shipment of crystal glassware under our purchase order ♯1234. Upon examining the merchandise, I found that one of the twelve vases was broken.

Therefore, I ask that you immediately replace this damaged merchandise. In the meantime, please tell us what to do with the damaged goods. I will await your prompt response. Thank you.

Words and Expressions

1. crystal glassware 水晶玻璃器皿
2. upon examining the merchandise 经过检查商品
3. vases 装饰瓶；花瓶
4. replace 替换
5. damaged merchandise/goods 损坏的商品

13-2　包装不全而导致的商品污损

Upon inspection of your shipment under our order ♯33099, we discovered that the merchandise in every box had been damaged by water, and is no longer sellable. This damage must have been caused by poor packaging at your site. We are enclosing our surveyors report on the damage.

We ask you to take immediate action to rectify the situation. Thank you.

Words and Expressions

1. upon inspection of 检查后
2. sellable 适于销售的
3. poor packaging 不良包装
4. surveyors 测量员
5. take immediate action 立刻采取行动
6. rectify 改正；校正

13-3　收到和订单不同的商品(1)

We have received our order POHB 9167 for CD players. Upon examination, however, we found the merchandise is not acceptable.

Please send the correct merchandise by air as soon as possible. Meanwhile, we will return the old shipment at your expense. Thank you.

Words and Expressions

1. upon examination 经检查
2. acceptable 能够接受的
3. correct 正确的；合适的
4. the old shipment 旧货
5. at your expense 由你方负担费用

13-4 收到和订单不同的商品(2)

To our great dismay, we discovered that the ten nose wheel tires for the Boeing 747 which arrived yesterday are the wrong type. Since time is of the essence, please send our order of model type MC 72002 by air freight immediately.

Any further delay in this critical shipment may cause us great financial loss. At the same time, we will await your instructions on how to return the wrong shipment back to you. Thank you.

Words and Expressions

1. to our great dismay 令我们非常沮丧的是
2. nose wheel tires 前轮轮胎（指飞机）
3. be of the essence 至关重要的
4. delay 延迟；耽搁；推延
5. critical 批评的；爱挑剔的；关键的；严重的
6. great financial loss 巨大的经济损失
7. instruction 指示，指令

13-5 交货商品数量不足

We received the shipment of our order for 88 oak chairs and inspected it at our warehouse. To our dismay, we found only 55 chairs, 33 short of the number we ordered.

Please explain this discrepancy. At any rate, please arrange immediate delivery of the remainder of our order. We await your prompt reply. Thank you.

Words and Expressions

1. dismay 沮丧，失望
2. oak chairs 橡木椅
3. warehouse 仓库；货栈；批发商店
4. discrepancy 矛盾；不符合

5. remainder 剩余部分

6. at any rate 无论如何

13-6 支票支付的商品未到

On November 28, I sent you my check for $47.88 with my purchase order for an all-weather duffel bag, advertised in *Sunrise magazine*. Today, after five weeks, I have received neither the merchandise nor an acknowledgment of my order.

Please check your records and let me know what is delaying the delivery. If you are unable to fill this order immediately, please consider my order canceled, and return the payment.

Your prompt attention to this matter is requested. Thank you.

Words and Expressions

1. check 支票(名词), 检查(动词)
2. an all-weather 全天候的
3. duffel bag 露营帆布包
4. advertised in Sunrise magazine 在《日出》杂志上登广告
5. acknowledgment 承认；承认书；
6. fill this order 履行/完成这笔订单
7. cancel 取消

13-7 大幅延长交货时间导致的解除合同警告

Subject: Our order for 1 000 Super Saver Shower Heads

Regarding the above, we have yet to receive a notice of shipment from you. It has been 60 days since we submitted the order. Please be reminded of the 30 days delivery term in the contract.

If you fail to execute shipment within the next 10 days, we will be obliged to cancel this order.

Words and Expressions

1. saver shower heads 储水淋浴喷头
2. a notice of shipment 发送通知
3. submitt the order 提交订单
4. be reminded of 提醒
5. execute 执行
6. within 在内；在里面；不超过

7. be obliged to 被迫，不得不

13-8 没按期交货而取消订单

We regret to have learned that you failed to ship our order via MSC. Since you could not ensure delivery here by October 31, 2019, the absolute deadline we agreed upon, we must cancel this order.

We will contact you shortly to discuss how this situation can best be resolved.

Words and Expressions

1. via 经由，通过
2. MSC 地中海航运的简称
3. ensure 确保；担保
4. absolute 绝对的，完全的
5. deadline 最后期限，截止期限
6. resolve 下定决心，解决问题

小知识

MSC

MSC，全称是 Mediterranean Shipping Company（中文名：地中海航运公司），总部位于瑞士日内瓦。

MSC 于 1970 年建立，2007 年成为按照集装箱运力和集装箱船数量排序的世界第二大航运公司，业务网络遍布世界各地。20 世纪 70 年代，地中海航运专注发展非洲及地中海之间的航运服务。至 1985 年，地中海航运拓展业务到欧洲，及后更开办大西洋航线。从投资规模已可看到地中海航运的热诚及其发展的速度。MSC 在全世界有 350 个机构，28 000 员工，255 艘集装箱船，880 000 TEU 的运力，在全球五大洲 215 个码头停靠，提供 175 条直航和组合航线服务。

13-9 处理对缺陷商品的投诉

Thank you for your letter of March 20, 2019. We regret that you are not happy with the camera you purchased from us.

Judging from your description, it is apparently defective merchandise. Please return it to us together with the receipt, and we will be happy to replace it with a new one.

We apologize for any inconvenience this may have caused.

Words and Expressions

1. purchase 购买;采购
2. judge from 从……判断
3. description 描述;形容
4. apparently 似乎;看来;显然
5. defective merchandise 缺陷商品
6. receipt 收据;发票
7. replace 替换
8. apologize for 为……道歉;替……道歉
9. any inconvenience this may have caused 由此而带来的不便

13-10 拒绝对破损商品的赔偿要求

This is in reply to your letter of April 8, 2019. Upon checking our records, we found no fault in our packing methods. We have always employed standard export packing and have had no problems in the past. We strongly feel that the damage was caused by the shipper. Therefore, we suggest that you contact your insurance agent about your claim.

We are sorry about this incident and hope that you find a satisfactory solution. If you have any questions, please contact us. Thank you.

Words and Expressions

1. in reply to 针对……的答复
2. upon checking our records 在检查我们的记录的基础上
3. fault 错误
4. method 方法;条理
5. standard 标准;规格
6. incident 事件;事故
7. a satisfactory solution 令人满意的解决办法
8. insurance agent 保险代理
9. claim 投诉,赔偿

13-11 对未交货商品的催促

I received my order of a Posh crystal bowl in good condition, for which I thank you. However, I am puzzled to find with it a crystal flower ornament, and an additional charge was added on the invoice.

I have neither recollection nor records of ordering any other items but the crystal bowl. Please reverse the charge to my credit account immediately. I will keep the extra merchandise here pending instructions from you.

Words and Expressions

1. posh crystal bowl 高档水晶碗
2. be puzzled to 困惑于
3. an additional charge 追加费用
4. ornament 装饰；装饰物
5. recollection 记忆；追忆；往事
6. pending 直到；在等待……期间
7. reverse 撤销，推翻

13-12 指出发票金额错误

We have found a discrepancy between our records and your invoice ♯12233. Our records based on your price list show that the amount should be $355,980.00.

Please check your records and reissue a corrected invoice so that we may make payment. Thank you.

Words and Expressions

1. discrepancy 矛盾；不符合（之处）
2. reissue 再版；重新发行
3. corrected 修正的

13-13 要求退回重复支付的货款

According to my records, the Principal Medical Fund paid you $175.00 for the treatment I received on January 11, 2019. In the meantime, I also paid $175.00 for the same service per my check ♯730, dated March 4, 2019.

Therefore, please refund the $175.00 over payment as soon as possible. If you have any questions or if your records do not agree, please contact me as soon as possible. Thank you.

Words and Expressions

1. the Principal Medical Fund 主要医疗基金
2. in the meantime 同时；与此同时
3. refund 资金偿还；退还

  4. over payment 多付；超额偿付，超付

  5. not agree 不一致

13－14 订正支付款金额

  Thank you for your payment of ＄56,660.00 per your check ♯1090. We assume this payment was made for our invoice ♯19344 for the amount of ＄560.00. If so, you have overpaid by ＄660.

  We are crediting the difference to your account, which will be reflected on the next statement. If you would like us to return the over payment, please instruct us accordingly. Thank you.

Words and Expressions

  1. assume 假定；认为

  2. overpaid 多付给(某人)钱

  3. crediting the difference 支付差额

  4. be reflected on 反映，反思

  5. statement （文字）陈述；结算单

  6. accordingly 因此；于是；依据

13－15 寄错的催款书

  Much to our surprise, we received your collection letter dated September 24, 2019. Our records show that our account has been paid in full since July 5. We assume you will find that this was your clerical error. If not, please get back to us, and we will forward you a copy of the canceled check.

  In the meantime, we would appreciate receiving your corrected statement.

Words and Expressions

  1. much to our surprise 非常惊讶

  2. collection letter 索款信，拖欠债务催告信

  3. clerical error 笔误；写错

  4. paid in full 已全额支付

  5. forward 发送

13－16 没有根据的货款支付请求书

  On May 14, 2019, I received a crystal bowl from you together with an invoice for ＄56.00. Inasmuch as I placed no such order, I believe this is an error on your part.

I will keep the merchandise here pending instructions from you.

Words and Expressions

1. inasmuch as 由于；因为
2. error 错误；过失
3. pending instructions 等待指令

13-17 错误的信用卡还款通知书

This is to inform you that my credit card has been charged erroneously for my recent purchase from your catalog.

I place an order for one dozen Rainbow Brand bras #33445 at $125.00 plus $22.00 shipping charge in early September. The total charge should have been $147.00, yet I was charged $231.37.

Please investigate your records and correct the error immediately. Thank you.

Words and Expressions

1. erroneously 错误；不正确
2. catalog 商品目录；目录册
3. investigate 调查；审查

13-18 商品质量的投诉

We have to report you one serious problem about spigot which imported from you this year.

There are three different customer complained the spigot is broken. It seems the material is not so good than before. Even though the price is raised, the quality is worse. Especially while lamp head is hung from ceiling, if the spigot is broken, the big accident (such as lamp head fall to floor to explore or hurt person in studio) will happen. It is very dangerous. We strongly ask you to check the material of spigot immediately.

Words and Expressions

1. serious problem 严重的问题
2. spigot 栓；龙头；套管
3. lamp head 灯头
4. hung from 挂在天花板上
5. fall to floor to explore 掉到地上爆炸

13-19 收到与样品不同质量的商品投诉

We would like to draw your attention to the defective goods shipped by the Steamship "Sunlight" on October, 20.

Upon unpacking the consignment, to our great disappointment, we found that the quality was much inferior to the sample on which we approved the order.

We are now in a very awkward situation, because our customers, who have been very strict about the quality, are very impatient to take delivery of goods.

We hope that you will immediately take this matter into your careful consideration. Your early reply will be most appreciated.

Words and Expressions

1. steamship 汽船；大轮船
2. awkward 令人尴尬的
3. consignment 装运的货物；托运
4. inferior to 次于；不如
5. impatient to take delivery of goods 迫不及待地接受货物

Exercise

Ⅰ. Fill in the blanks with the following words.

| reverse | than | deadline | goods | shipment |
| keep | worse | situation | via | replace |

1. I have received your _____ of crystal glassware under our purchase order #1234.
2. Therefore, I ask that you immediately _____ this damaged merchandise.
3. In the meantime, please tell us what to do with the damaged _____.
4. We regret to have learned that you failed to ship our order _____ MSC.
5. Since you could not ensure delivery here by October 31, 2019, the absolute _____ we agreed upon, we must cancel this order.
6. We will contact you shortly to discuss how this _____ can best be resolved.
7. It seems the material is not so good _____ before.
8. Even though the price is raised, the quality is _____.
9. Please _____ the charge to my credit account immediately.
10. I will _____ the extra merchandise here pending instructions from you.

Ⅱ. Translate the following words and phrases.

Section A：Translate into English.

1. 缺陷商品

2. 解除合同

3. 投诉

4. 破损商品

5. 数量不足

Section B：Translate into Chinese.

1. investigate

2. a very awkward situation

3. great financial loss

4. reissue a corrected invoice

5. make payment

Ⅲ. Writing in English.

请给你的海外进口商写一封交货商品数量不足的投诉函。

14　Quotation
　　预　算

Aims to Obtain

Upon completion of the unit，you should：

- know how to require the quotaion；
- be able to make good use of the words or expressions to reply on quotaion.

14－1　要求出示预算表

Reliant Uniforms Co., Ltd. has long served many reputable companies in China，and we would like the opportunity to submit a quote for your company uniforms.

Because we consider it important to design the uniform to best suit your needs and taste，we would like to meet with you to gather some necessary information. I will call you in a few days to schedule an appointment.

We will be happy to supply references upon request.

Thank you.

Words and Expressions

1. reputable 值得尊敬的，声誉好的
2. gather 收集
3. supply references upon request 应要求提供参考资料

14-2　要求报预算价

We obtained a couple of your brochures at the Camdex Show in San Francisco. We would like you to quote your most competitive price for 100 of your laser printers, Model MP-130, to be shipped from FOB Oakland in the middle of September, 2019. We also need information on payment terms.

We look forward to doing business with you shortly.

Thank you.

Words and Expressions

1. obtain 获得
2. brochures 小册子
3. quote 报价（国际贸易专业用语）
4. most competitive price 最有竞争力的价格
5. laser printers 激光打印机
6. FOB 离岸价（国际贸易术语）
7. Oakland 奥克兰（位于美国西海岸的加利福尼亚州，是加州人口第8大城市）
8. payment terms 支付条件

14-3　对预算价的回复及再度报价

It is a pleasure to send you the information you requested, and we are happy that you are considering our company in connection with your plan to purchase your office supplies.

As you will see from the enclosed material, we offer a broad range of merchandise and our prices are very competitive. If you need more information or assistance, please let us know. We could also arrange to have a sales representative to visit you.

Thank you for the opportunity to submit a quote. We look forward to doing business with you in the near future.

Words and Expressions

1. in connection with 有关……
2. office supplies 办公用品
3. a broad range of merchandise 广范围的商品
4. sales representative 销售代表

Exercise

Ⅰ. Fill in the blanks with the following words.

| schedule | terms | submit |

1. We would like the opportunity to _____ a quote for your company uniforms.
2. I will call you in a few days to _____ an appointment.
3. We also need information on payment _____.

Ⅱ. Translate the following words and phrases.

Section A：Translate into English.

1. 提供参考
2. 报预算价
3. 有竞争力的价格

Section B：Translate into Chinese.

1. schedule an appointment
2. FOB
3. a sales representative

15 Business Negotiation
交易蹉商

Aims to Obtain

Upon completion of the unit, you should：

- know how to write letters negotiating about trading terms with foreign business partners；
- be able to make good use of the words or expressions to write counter-offer, such as request of discount, etc.；
- grasp some basic tactics about writing acceptance.

15-1 支付条件

Thank you for sending us a quote in response to our interest in your module kitchens.

We are impressed by the innovative design of your products. The delivery time is also acceptable. However, we are hesitant to place an order because we feel the payment terms you ask are too strict.

If you can offer us more lenient terms, it is our intention to place an order immediately.

Words and Expressions

1. in response to 对……做出的反应/回答
2. module 模块;组件
3. module kitchens 整体厨房
4. be impressed by 被……所感动;对……印象深刻
5. innovative 革新的;创新的
6. be hesitant to 犹豫不决
7. lenient 宽大的;仁慈的
8. intention 意图;目的;意向

15-2 降价(1)

Thank you for offering to us your Zola Brand tennis shoes. Your prices, however, seem to be about 10% higher compared to those of better known brands. In order to compete favorably on the market, your prices must be reduced at least 15 percent.

If you can agree to our suggested pricing strategy, we would like to order 2000 pairs. We await your reply.

Words and Expressions

1. favorably 顺利地;有利地
2. reduced 减少的;简化的
3. strategy 战略性对策

15-3 降价(2)

We are planning to purchase a large quantity of your fireproof outdoor house paint. Before we place an order, however, we would like to know what sort of volume discounts you might offer. Our projected need is 10,000 gallons for immediate delivery. Our standard form of payment is an irrevocable letter of credit.

Your prompt reply will be appreciated.

Words and Expressions

1. fireproof 使防火；使耐火
2. sort of 种类
3. volume 量；大量
4. gallons 加仑
5. irrevocable 不能取消的；不可改变的
6. letter of credit 信用证（简称 L/C）

15-4 条件变更

Regarding your auto CD player, we feel the term of your warranty should be extended to five years. Such an extended warranty is necessary for your product to compete favorably with other better known brands, at least until we succeed in penetrating the tight market further.

We hope you agree with us on this point. We look forward to your reply. Thank you.

Words and Expressions

1. extend 延长，延期
2. the term of warranty 保修期
3. penetrate 渗透；贯穿
4. the tight market 紧缩的市场

15-5 接受请求

We received your letter of May 15, 2019, requesting more lenient payment terms. In consideration of your excellent payment record in the past, we are pleased to comply with your request. For all future purchases we agree to accept 10% down, with the balance to be paid within 30 days of delivery.

We look forward to doing more business with you.

Thank you.

Words and Expressions

1. lenient 宽大的；仁慈的

2. in consideration of 考虑到；由于

3. comply with 服从；遵从

15-6 拒绝打折要求

Thank you for your inquiry regarding a volume discount on our fireproof outdoor house paint. Inasmuch as our prices are regulated by the manufacturer, we are unable to offer any prices other than those posted.

Although we cannot accommodate your request for a discount, we are sure that you will be pleased with the excellence of our product. Thank you for understanding our position.

Words and Expressions

1. inquiry 询问
2. fireproof 防火
3. inasmuch as 由于；因为
4. be regulated 受管制
5. those posted 那些公布的（价格）
6. accommodate 容纳；使适应

15-7 要求支付期限延长

Due to unexpected financial difficulties, we are forced to request a postponement on the payment due date for invoice #28675. It looks as though we will be able to pay in full by September 1, 2019.

We will, of course, do our best to pay this off sooner if at all possible. Your understanding is most sincerely appreciated. Thank you.

Words and Expressions

1. unexpected 想不到；意外的
2. financial difficulties 财政困难
3. be forced to 被迫做某事
4. postponement 延期；推迟
5. payment due date 支付期限

15-8 答应支付期限延长

We received your letter of August 10, 2019 requesting postponement of the payment due date for the outstanding balance due us.

While our policy is to avoid delinquent receivables as much as possible, we also want to do what we can to assist our valued customers whenever necessary. For this reason we have approved your request for delayed payment until December 15, 2019.

> **Words and Expressions**

1. outstanding 未支付的
2. delinquent receivables 拖欠的应收款项
3. assist 帮助
4. approve your request 核准、认可你的要求(答应你的诉求)

15-9 拒绝支付期限延长

We received your letter requesting an extension on the payment due date, but we regret to inform you that we are unable to accommodate your request, as our business, too, is operated on a tight cash flow. Therefore, your payments will be expected as scheduled.

Thank you for understanding our situation.

> **Words and Expressions**

1. accommodate 容纳;使适应,答应(要求)
2. a tight cash flow 紧缺的现金流
3. as scheduled 如期;按照预定时间

15-10 对手续费涨价的交涉

We are writing you regarding our sales commission. As you know, in recent years competition in the Chinese jewelry market has become extremely intense. In order to maintain the targeted level of sales, we have had to increase our advertising expenses by about 20% in the last six months. Therefore, in order to maintain the targeted level of sales, we have had to increase our advertising expenses by about 20% in the last six months. Therefore, in order to maintain our position as your effective agent, we must ask you to increase our commission rate to fifteen percent as soon as possible.

We hope you understand the conditions necessitating this action. Thank you.

> **Words and Expressions**

1. commission 手续费;佣金

2. Chinese jewelry market 中国珠宝市场
3. extremely 极度地
4. intense 强烈
5. advertising expenses 广告费
6. necessitating this action 采取此措施的必要

15-11 中断谈判

We feel that our good-faith efforts to negotiate with you during the past five months regarding technical collaboration have not been properly reciprocated by your company, and we are forced to conclude that there are irreconcilable differences in our objectives. Therefore, we are terminating our discussions with you as of this writing. Thank you.

Words and Expressions

1. good-faith 有诚信的
2. technical collaboration 技术合作
3. reciprocated by 被……作为回报
4. conclude 下结论
5. irreconcilable 不可调和的
6. terminatie our discussions 结束我们之间的谈判

Exercise

Ⅰ. Fill in the blanks with the following words.

| Hesitant | competition | regarding | assist |
| delinquent | innovative | maintain | warranty |

1. We are impressed by the _____ design of your products.
2. However, we are _____ to place an order because we feel the payment terms you ask are too strict.
3. Regarding your auto CD player, we feel the term of your _____ should be extended to five years.
4. As you know, in recent years in the Chinese jewelry market _____ has become extremely intense.
5. In order to _____ the targeted level of sales, we have had to increase our advertising expenses by about 20% in the last six months.
6. We are writing you _____ our sales commission.

7. While our policy is to avoid _____ receivables as much as possible.

8. We also want to do what we can to _____ our valued customers whenever necessary.

II. **Translate the following words and phrases.**

Section A：Translate into English.

1. 手续费

2. 支付期限

3. 打折

Section B：Translate into Chinese.

1. pricing strategy

2. increase our advertising expenses

3. excellent payment record

16 Apology
道　歉

Aims to Obtain

Upon completion of the unit，you should：

- know how to write letters about apology;
- be able to make good use of the words or expressions to write aplogy due to bill mistake，etc..

16-1　对没有遵守约定的道歉

　　I want to apologize for having to cancel our plans for next weekend at the last moment. I know you have put so much work into preparing for the dinner party, and I was looking forward to meeting your friends. I feel very bad about being forced to fly to London on urgent business and cancel our plans at the last minute.

　　Flowers are on the way. I hope they will help ease the disappointment. Let's make plans to do something special after I return.

　　I truly am sorry.

　　Love,

Words and Expressions

1. be forced to 被迫做某事
2. urgent business 紧急事务
3. on the way 在途中
4. ease 缓解
5. disappointment 失望；扫兴

16-2 对没有及时回信的道歉

I'm sorry I haven't written you for a while. Things have been hectic, but I realize that is no excuse. Please let me know how you are doing.

Words and Expressions

1. for a while 一段时间
2. hectic 繁忙的；忙乱的
3. realize 意识到
4. excuse 理由，借口

16-3 对账单错误的道歉

We apologize for the recent error we made in sending you a collection letter.
The statement should have shown a "zero balance" in the account. Please accept our apology. We have taken precautions to prevent a repeat of this kind of error. Thank you.

Words and Expressions

1. error 错误
2. apology 道歉认错
3. precautions 预防措施
4. prevent a repeat of 防止……的重演

Exercise

Ⅰ. Fill in the blanks with the following words.

| apologize | error | ease |

1. We apologize for the recent _____ we made in sending you a collection letter.
2. Flowers are on the way. I hope they will help _____ the disappointment.

3. I want to _____ for having to cancel our plans for next weekend at the last moment.

Ⅱ. **Translate the following words and phrases.**

Section A：Translate into English.

1. 接受道歉
2. 防止重新出错

Section B：Translate into Chinese.

1. disappointment
2. no excuse

17　Visiting
　　　探　望

Aims to Obtain

Upon completion of the unit, you should：
- know how to write letters about visiting;
- be able to make good use of the words or expressions to write going to see patients, friends or family involved in a traffic accident, etc..

17-1　探望病人

I am very sorry to hear that you are ill. I only hope it is not too serious and you will recover soon. Please be assured that you have nothing to worry about at work. Just relax and get plenty of rest. If there is anything I can do to help, please call me.

I look forward to seeing you healthy again and back to work very soon.

Words and Expressions

1. recover 恢复
2. relax 放松
3. be assured 安心,放心
4. get plenty of rest 充分休息

17-2　回复探望

Thank you for your concern while I was ill. My doctor says I am completely well now and I have returned to work.

While I was confined to my bed, it was very comforting to know of your concern for me. Thank you again.

Words and Expressions

1. concern 关心，关注
2. be confined to 禁闭；限于
3. comforting 令人欣慰的；安慰的

17-3 探望事故家庭

I was very sorry to hear about your daughter being involved in a traffic accident. I can find no adequate words to express consolation, and I become choked up inside when I think how hard it must be for you.

I will be praying for her quick and complete recovery.

Words and Expressions

1. be involved 被卷入……
2. adequate 贴切的；适当的
3. consolation 安慰；慰问
4. choke up 因感情冲动说不出话来
5. be praying for 为……祈求，为……祈祷
6. quick and complete recovery 早日痊愈

17-4 探望受灾友人

My wife and I have been concerned since we heard of the fire in your area last week, we sincerely hope that your home and family were not directly involved, or if there was any damage, that it is minimal.

Please remember that we are thinking of you. If there is anything we can do to help you. Please let us know.

Words and Expressions

1. fire 火灾
2. minimal 最小的；极少的
3. be not directly involved 没有直接卷入

17-5 探望受灾客户

We were all very saddened to hear about the tragedy your business experienced recently. It is hard to believe this accident has upset your business so drastically overnight. However, we believe that you have the courage, hope and resources to bring your business back to normal very soon.

Please be assured that we will do whatever we can to assist you for a quick recovery. We are interested in continuing our valued business relationship with you for into the future.

Words and Expressions

1. tragedy 悲剧;惨剧
2. upset 打乱,搅乱
3. drastically 大大地;彻底地;激烈地
4. be assured that 请放心

Exercise

Ⅰ. Fill in the blanks with the following words.

| upset | normal | concern | accident | recovery |

1. While I was confined to my bed, it was very comforting to know of your _____ for me.
2. I will be praying for her quick and complete _____.
3. I was very sorry to hear about your daughter being involved in a traffic _____.
4. It is hard to believe this accident has _____ your business so drastically overnight.
5. However, we believe that you have the courage, hope and resources to bring your business back to _____ very soon.

Ⅱ. Translate the following words and phrases.

Section A: Translate into English.

1. 交通事故
2. 康复
3. 充分休息

Section B: Translate into Chinese.

1. return to work

2. minimal

3. the fire in your area

18 Condolences
慰　问

> **Aims to Obtain**
> **Upon completion of the unit, you should:**
> • know how to write letters about greetings for people falling in trouble;

> • be able to make good use of the words or expressions to write the deepest sympathy for people who lost relatives.

18-1 慰问失去亲人的家庭(1)

We were so very sad to hear of Raymond's death. Our hearts go out to you at this very difficult time. We know the last few months were a struggle for him, and now he is resting in peace.

We want you to know that we will be here for you in the months ahead, we would like to call you soon to see how we can help. Our love and prayers are with you.

Words and Expressions

1. our hearts go out to you 我们的心与你同在
2. struggle 搏斗；奋斗；努力
3. in peace 平安地，安静地

18-2 慰问失去亲人的家庭(2)

I was very sorry to hear about the loss of your husband, it is very sad to lose someone so close. Although this may be the time when there is little anyone can do to ease your pain, I wanted you to know that you have my deepest sympathy.

If there is any I can help, please let me know.

Words and Expressions

1. lose someone so close 失去如此亲近的人

2. ease your pain 减轻你的痛苦

3. deepest sympathy 最深切的同情

18-3 慰问失去亲人的客户

It was with both shock and sorrow that I learned of the sudden death of Mr. Chaplin. As he had long been a great leader for the company, his death must be a big loss to you all. He will be missed, both by us and by the many other people who had the pleasure of knowing him,

I extend my deepest condolences to you.

Words and Expressions

1. shock and sorrow 震惊与悲伤
2. great leader 杰出的领导
3. big loss 重大损失
4. extend my deepest condolences 给予最沉痛的哀悼

18-4 回复慰问

My children and I thank you for your kind condolences upon the death of my wife. It was a great shock to all of us, and we are still deep in mourning. But knowing that we have friends who are so caring and thoughtful is most comforting.

Thank you again for your expression of sympathy.

Words and Expressions

1. condolences 同情；吊唁
2. great shock 大为震惊
3. deep in mourning 深深的哀悼
4. sympathy 同情；同感；慰问

Exercise

Ⅰ. Fill in the blanks with the following words.

| with | ease | struggle | loss | shock |

1. We know the last few months were a _____ for him, and now he is resting in peace.
2. Our love and prayers are _____ you.
3. I was very sorry to hear about the _____ of your husband, it is very sad to lose someone so close.

4. It was a great _____ to all of us, and we are still deep in mourning.
5. Although this may be the time when there is little anyone can do to _____ your pain, I wanted you to know that you have my deepest sympathy.

Ⅱ. **Translate the following words and phrases.**

Section A: Translate into English.

1. 巨大的损失
2. 安静休息
3. 哀悼

Section B: Translate into Chinese.

1. a great shock
2. deepest condolences
3. sympathy

Unit 3

Common Business E-mail Collection
常用商务 E-mail 案例集

> **Aims to Obtain**
>
> **Upon completion of the unit, you should:**
>
> - know how to write E-mail;
> - be familiar with the words or expressions to write various contents;
> - be familiar with air express service such as UPS, DHL, etc..

▶ 1　Landing a Dream Job
　　　找到理想的工作

Subject: Landing a Dream Job!

Hi Nick,

　　I want you to be the first person to know that I've been offered a dream job at Ridge Corp. in Hartford. My new employment will start on November 1. Once I'm settled down in the new place, I'll write you again with my new address, etc..

Words and Expressions

1. Hartford 哈特福德（美国康涅狄格州首府）
2. employment 雇用；职业
3. a dream job 理想的工作

143

2　My Visit to San Francisco
　　访问旧金山

Subject：My Visit to San Francisco

Pete and Jean，

　　Guess what! I will be flying to San Francisco on business next month. Could I see you and possibly stay in your home for a couple of days? I will arrive at SFO via JAL 003 on the morning of September 15，and depart for Boston on the 18th. As I have a business commitment on the 17th，I am wondering if I could visit you on the first two days.

　　Please let me know ASAP if this schedule works out for you. Also，tell me what goodies you want me to bring. Oh，I'm so excited and can't wait to see you and your family.

Words and Expressions

　　1. SFO 旧金山国际机场（San Francisco International Airport）代码，由 IATA（国际航空运输协会）制定的代码

　　2. JAL 003 日本航空003号航班

　　3. a couple of days 几天

　　4. commitment 承诺；许诺

　　5. goodies 特别吸引人的东西；美味的食品

3　Response for Visit to San Francisco
　　回复来访旧金山

Subject：Re：Your Visit to San Francisco

Hi Xiaojuan WANG，

　　We are all so happy to hear that you're visiting San Francisco next month. You are more than welcome to stay with us as long as you can. It's very nice of you to ask us what we want from China，but your smiling face is all that we want. We will be waiting for your arrival at SFO.

Words and Expressions

　　1. Re 关于……（regarding 的缩写形式）

　　2. more than welcome 热烈欢迎

144

3. stay with us as long as you can 在我们家里作客，随便你住多久都行

4　Change of My E-mail Address
　　邮箱地址变更

Subject：Change of My E-mail Address

Dear all，

Please note that as of October 1, I will change my E-mail address as I've been receiving too much junk mail lately. The new address is Luke007@sophitel.com. Please keep me in touch.

Words and Expressions

1. note that 请注意；
2. as of 现在，从……
3. junk mail 垃圾邮件
4. Keep sb. in touch 与某人保持联系

5　Finding a Host Family
　　寻找寄宿家庭

Subject：Do Me a Favor? /Finding a Host Family

Dear Mr. and Mrs. Stanford：

My friendly greetings from Shanghai. I hope you and your family are well. Today I have a favor to ask you. An eighteen-year-old daughter of one of my colleagues hopes to spend this summer studying English in a school in Oakland while staying with a family. Do you know any families who may be interested in hosting her? She'd be able to pay for room and board. Please let me know if you think you can help her find a host family.

Words and Expressions

1. a Host Family 寄宿家庭，一般指学生寒暑假在海外学习时，提供住宿的家庭
2. greetings from 来自……的问候
3. have a favor 需要帮个忙，有个请求
4. colleague 同事
5. Oakland 奥克兰（美国加利福尼亚州西部港市）
6. pay for room and board 支付住宿与伙食费

6 Mail-order Catalog
邮购的商品目录

Subject: Mail-order Catalog

Dear sirs,

I recently saw your mail-order catalog featuring apparel for young adults. Do you accept direct orders from China? If so, please send me a copy of your current catalog, with information on payment methods and delivery time. I look forward to hearing from you soon.

Words and Expressions

1. featuring 主要描述,以……为特征
2. apparel 衣物;服装
3. adults 成年人
4. current 现在的;最近的
5. payment methods 付款方法
6. delivery time 发货时间

7 My Order for the Everflo Baby Carriage
订购 Everflo 牌婴儿手推车

Subject: My Order for the Everflo Baby Carriage

Dear Sales Manager:

I placed an order with you for the following merchandise about a month ago, but I have neither received it nor heard anything from you. Please get back to me on the status of my order as soon as possible. Thank you for your attention.

Merchandise: One Everflo Baby Carriage; Sunrise Model

Words and Expressions

1. Everflo Baby Carriage 艾弗洛婴儿车
2. neither...nor 没有……也没有
3. get back to 答复;反馈
4. status 情况,状态

8 Reply on Your Order of Baby Carriage
回复订购婴儿手推车

Subject：Re：Reply on Your Order of Baby Carriage

Ms. Shimoda：

Thank you for your inquiry about your purchase order for our Everflo baby carriage. Our record shows that we shipped your order on September 20 by UPS. If you do not receive it by the end of this month，please notify us immediately. Thank you for your patience.

Words and Expressions

1. inquiry 调查；审查；询问
2. record 记录；记载；标明
3. notify 通知；布告

小知识

UPS

UPS(United Parcel Service)，美国联合包裹快递。于1907年作为一家信使公司成立于美国华盛顿州西雅图，是一家全球性的公司，其商标是世界知名商标之一。作为世界上最大的快递承运商与包裹递送公司，同时也是运输、物流、资本与电子商务服务的领导性的提供者，UPS每天都在世界上200多个国家和地域管理着物流、资金流与信息流。通过结合货物流、信息流和资金流，UPS不断开发供应链管理、物流和电子商务的新领域，如今UPS已发展成拥有300亿美元资产的大公司。

2017年6月7日，2017年《财富》美国500强排行榜发布，UPS快递排名第46位。2017年6月，《2017年BrandZ最具价值全球品牌100强》公布，UPS快递排名第16位。

9 Job Application with Resume
附有简历的工作申请

Subject：Job Application with Resume

Dear Director of Human Resources：

While visiting your web site，I noticed an open position for a graphic designer with minimum one-year experience in CAD. The position also requires language

147

skills in both English and Japanese. I feel I am well qualified and wish to apply for this position with my attached resume.

I am hoping that I will have an opportunity to be interviewed by you at an early date. Thank you for your attention.

Words and Expressions

1. an open position 空的职位
2. a graphic designer 一个平面设计师
3. minimum 最少,至少
4. CAD 计算机辅助设计
5. well qualified 很有资格,符合条件
6. attached resume 附上的简历
7. be interviewed by 接受……采访

10 Inviting to Job Interview
工作面试的通知

Subject: Inviting to Job Interview

Ms. Boom,

Thank you for your application for the position of mechanical draftsperson. We have reviewed your resume and you seem to have the skills and experience we are looking for. As the next step in the process, we would like to meet you in person and learn more about you.

Please contact me at (650-444-5467) as soon as you receive this message. I am looking forward to meeting you.

Words and Expressions

1. interview 面试
2. application 申请
3. mechanical draftsperson 机械绘图员
4. in the process 在这个过程中
5. in person 亲自,单独

11 Confirm an Appointment
确认预约

Subject: Confirm an Appointment

Mr. Fong,

This is to confirm the appointment I've just made with you on the telephone. I will be meeting you in the lobby of the Mayflower Hotel in downtown Los Angeles at 4:00 p.m. on November 2nd. If any changes are necessary, you can reach me at this E-mail address between now and then. I'm looking forward to meeting you soon.

Words and Expressions

1. confirm an appointment 预约的确认
2. in the lobby 在大厅里；前厅
3. Mayflower Hotel in downtown 市中心的五月花酒店
4. reach sb. 联系某人

12 Requesting a Meeting
请求面谈

Subject: Requesting a Meeting

Ms. Chrysler, General Manager,

As a new regional sales manager at Huawei Corporation of America, my first priority is getting acquainted with companies like yours in Northern California. I will be in your area during the first week of October and would appreciate a few minutes of your time. I would like to find out more about your business and at the same time show you our line of products.

I will be calling you soon to see if we can schedule an appointment. Thank you.

Best Regards,

Words and Expressions

1. regional 区域的；地区
2. priority 优先；优先权
3. get acquainted with 结交，认识
4. schedule an appointment 约定面会时间
5. Best Regards 致敬；最好的祝福（结尾敬语，一般在文章结束时用）

13 Thanks for a Warm Reception
感谢热情接待

Subject：Thanks for Warm Reception

Dear Dr. Huchinson：

Thank you very much for talking time to meet Dr. Kobayashi and me last week. We are very happy that the preliminary discussion about our technical collaboration went very well. We also enjoyed the time with you over lunch at the seafood restaurant on the waterfront.

Please be assured that we will work hard to materialize the project we discussed with you and your staff. We will keep you posted on progress.

Words and Expressions

1. preliminary 初步的；初级的
2. technical collaboration 技术协会；技术合作
3. seafood 海鲜；海产食品
4. waterfront 海滨；江边；
5. be assured that 确信；确保
6. Materialize 具体化；实质化
7. keep you posted on progress 随时告诉你进展情况

14 Team Meeting on Project Z
有关项目 Z 的团队会议

Subject：Team Meeting on Project Z

Fellow Team Members：

Please make your calendar for our team meeting this coming Friday at 3 p.m. in conference room #101. Each member has five minutes to report his or her progress on assignments and present any other issues at the meeting. Since we will be on a tight schedule，don't be late.

Words and Expressions

1. calendar 日历；日程表
2. conference room 会议室
3. assignments 分配的任务；工作

4. present any other issues 提出任何其他问题

15 Clarification of Assigned Task
明确工作责任

Subject: Clarification of Assigned Task

Dear Vivian,

It is my understanding that at yesterday's meeting I was assigned to write up the documentation and specifications of the new product. Today, I found out Kenji Yokoyama believes that it is his task. Are we sharing the same assignment, or are we working on two different phases? Please clarify the matter since we both are confused.

Thank you.

Words and Expressions

1. documentation 记录；文档
2. specifications 说明书
3. clarify 使清楚；明确
4. right away 马上
5. confused 困惑的，混乱的

16 Request for Vacation
请求休假

Subject: Request for Vacation

Mr. King:

As per our conversation this morning, I am hereby submitting my written request for a two-week vacation from August 21 through September 1. During my absence, my colleague Ms. Nakamoto will be handling urgent problems. I will keep in touch with her on a regular basis. I appreciate your consideration.

Words and Expressions

1. hereby 特此；以此方式（一般用在特别正式的场合）
2. submit 提交
3. absence 缺勤；缺席
4. handling urgent problems 处理紧急问题

5. on a regular basis 经常；例行的；有规律的

17　I will be on Vacation
　　　休假通知

Subject：I'll be on Vacation

Dear Valued Clients：

　　From August 10 through August 20, I will be traveling to Australia on my vacation. During the period, Ms. Keiko Yamada, my capable colleague, will handle any urgent matters on my behalf. Thus, I hope my temporary absence from work won't affect your business needs. Keiko's address is Kyamada@nissando.co.jp. Thanks for your cooperation.

Words and Expressions

1. on Vacation 在度假中
2. clients 客户
3. during the period 在此期间
4. capable 能干的；有才能的
5. on my behalf 代表我
6. affect your business needs 影响你们的业务需求
7. temporary 暂时的，临时的

18　Interested in Your Services
　　　对公司的服务感兴趣

Subject：Interested in Your Services

Dear Marketing Director：

　　One of our business contacts has recommended your firm to us. Please send us information on your marketing services together with your fee schedule. We're particularly interested in marketing water sporting goods in Canada via direct mail.

　　Thank you for your prompt attention.

　　Our mailing address is as follows：

Shanxi Sports Products IMP/EXP Co., Ltd.

NO.345 ZHONGSHAN ROAD,

TAIYUAN, CHINA

Attn：Jackie Wang

Words and Expressions

1. recommend 推荐
2. fee schedule 价格表
3. particularly 特别;尤其;异乎寻常地
4. direct mail 直邮

19 Appreciate Your Referral
感谢对本公司的介绍

Subject: Appreciate Your Referral

Dear Ms. Washington:

Mr. Tom Norlan, Marketing Director of Net-Mart, contacted me this morning, and said that you gave him our name. He expressed an interest in our services, and we scheduled a meeting next week, hoping to develop some business out of it.

Thank you very much for the referral. I hope we'll be able to return the favor sometime in the future.

Warmest Regards,

Words and Expressions

1. referral 介绍;指引
2. scheduled a meeting 计划、安排会议
3. return the favor 回报,报答

20 Visit Our New Website
本公司的网页已刷新

Subject: Visit Our New Website

Friends:

We've recently renovated our web site, and it looks much more attractive. It's also more functional with lots of worthwhile information. Please visit us by simply clicking www.inksanyo.co.jp. If you have any suggestions that will allow us to serve you better, please let us know.

Words and Expressions

1. renovate 翻新;刷新;整修

2. worthwhile 有价值的

3. functional 功能的；有多种用途的

4. simply clicking 简单点击

Exercise

Ⅰ. Fill in the blanks with the following words.

| Vacation | down | junk | lobby | couple | appointment |
| Language | absence | status | materialize | host | on |

1. Once I'm settled _____ in the new place, I'll write you again with my new address, etc..
2. Could I see you and possibly stay in your home for a _____ of days?
3. I will change my E-mail address as I've been receiving too much _____ mail lately.
4. Please be assured that we will work hard to _____ the project we discussed with you and your staff.
5. We will keep you posted _____ progress.
6. As per our conversation this morning, I am hereby submitting my written request for a two-week _____ from August 21 through September 1.
7. Thus, I hope my temporary _____ from work won't affect your business needs.
8. Please let me know if you think you can help her find a _____ family.
9. The position also requires _____ skills in both English and Japanese.
10. This is to confirm the _____ I've just made with you on the telephone.
11. I will be meeting you in the _____ of the Mayflower Hotel.
12. Please get back to me on the _____ of my order as soon as possible.

Ⅱ. Translate the following words and phrases.

Section A: Translate into English.

1. 休假
2. 热情接待
3. 寄宿家庭
4. 工作责任
5. 刷新网页

Section B: Translate into Chinese.

1. worthwhile information
2. temporary absence
3. client
4. in conference room

5. new employment

Ⅲ. **Writing in English.**

1. 请给你的海外贸易伙伴写一封有关公司地址和邮箱地址变更的 E-mail。
2. 请给你所有的海外客户写一封公司春节休假通知的邮件。

Unit 4

Useful Sentence for Business E-mail
常用 E-mail 经典句案例集

> **Aims to Obtain**
>
> **Upon completion of the unit, you should:**
> - know how to write useful sentences for greetings;
> - be able to make good use of the expressions to write complimentary close, etc..

▶ 1 Usual Greetings
　　一般的问候

(1) How are you (doing)?

(2) How's everything going?

(3) It's been a long time.

(4) Long time no see.

(5) What are you up to?

(6) How do you do?

(7) How is it going these days?

(8) Are you OK recently?

(9) Hello, nice to meet you.

(10) Nice to see you again.

2 Greetings of Special Day
特别日子的问候

(1) Congratulations!

(2) Happy birthday!

(3) Merry Christmas!

(4) A Happy New Year!

(5) Wishing you a beautiful Holiday Season and a Happy New Year!

(6) May this year bring you success, happiness and health.

(7) Happy Valentine's Day!

(8) Wishing you a very special Thanksgiving Day.

(9) Hope 2019 will be the best year for you.

(10) Happy Chinese New Year (Spring Festival)!

(11) May the year of 2019 bring you joy, health and wealth!

3 Grateful Expression
谢礼表达

(1) Thank you so much for that wonderful gift you gave me. I really liked it.

(2) It was a great help for me.

(3) That's very kind of you to say so.

(4) We very much appreciate your kindness.

(5) I really appreciate it.

(6) I can't thank you enough.

(7) Thank you very much for your kind support.

(8) Thank you for your prompt reply.

(9) Your prompt reply would be highly appreciated.

(10) Many thanks for your kind and warm letter.

(11) We appreciate your kind help and everything you do for us.

(12) I am very sincerely grateful to you for your help during stay in your country.

4 Apologizing
赔礼道歉

(1) I'm sorry.

(2) Please forgive me.

(3) That's my fault.

(4) I'm sorry. I really didn't mean that.

(5) Sorry. I can't help you right now.

(6) I wish I could help you.

(7) I'm sorry I caused you so much trouble.

(8) I can't apologize to you enough.

(9) I apologize if I upset you.

(10) Will you please accept my apology?

(11) Sorry to trouble you.

(12) Let me apologize any inconvenience caused by our company.

5 Thanks for Replying
对回信的感谢

(1) Thank you for your E-mail of March 23rd.

(2) Thank you for your prompt reply.

(3) Thank you for letting me know your new address.

(4) Glad to hear from you.

(5) So sorry I didn't write back sooner.

(6) I'm glad to hear from you.

(7) It has taken me a long time to respond to you.

(8) You did a great job!

(9) You did it!

(10) Good for you!

(11) Thank you so much for your invitation.

(12) Your offer sounds very attractive. I'd like to hear the full details.

(13) If you are going to come to China，be sure to let me know your plans.

(14) This is in response to your E-mail requesting the right to use the picture I took.

(15) Thank you so much for your prompt reply.

6 Recent Situation
传达近况

(1) I've been doing okay these days.

(2) I saw a movie yesterday. It was a British film with Chinese subtitles.

(3) Your party sounds like so much fun. But I have already made plans for next weekend.

(4) My winter vacation was busy, but very enjoyable.

(5) Yesterday I forced myself to stay in my apartment to finish the report.

(6) School started about two weeks ago and I'm already ready for a vacation.

7 The Reception Invitation
招待邀请

(1) I would like to invite you to my birthday party.

(2) How about a drink this weekend?

(3) I want to take you out to dinner this Friday.

(4) If you don't have anything exciting to do, let's go out shopping.

(5) I'll try to arrange a nice restaurant for the party.

(6) Well, it seems we should make it some other time.

(7) Maybe we'd better take a rain check.

(8) We invite you to a restaurant for an informal dinner.

(9) We sincerely invite you to join the Speed Business Meeting at Hilton Hotel.

(10) We extended invitations to secret guests will join and share welcome cocktail party.

8 To Inform and Inquire
通知和询问

(1) I have good news for you.

(2) Just a quick note to tell you that the September 11th meeting was canceled.

(3) For more information, please open the attached file.

(4) Can I have some information on this matter?

(5) We are looking for a place to stay tonight. Do you have a list of cheap hotels?

(6) Could you give me information on the new Internet service, please?

(7) I need some information on how they work, including the advantages and disadvantages.

(8) Who on your staff can provide information about scholarships?

(9) I believe you will find my educational background suitable for the job.

(10) The contract has already been translated into Chinese and was mailed seven days ago.

9 Comfirming Information
确认信息

(1) Thanks for booking the ticket. I wonder if I can pay them with a credit card.

(2) Is it still possible to meet with your boss next week?

(3) If these new plans cause any trouble, don not hesitate to tell us.

(4) Don't forget to tell me your phone number.

(5) We can't meet you at the airport. Please give us a call as soon as possible.

(6) I need to confirm my reservation of hotel room.

(7) You've booked an economy round trip for Mr. Wang Ning whose passport number is G87654321.

(8) Your flight is Air France from Shanghai to Rio de Janeiro, which departure at 10:10 on August 3rd and returns on August 15th.

10 Requesting Help
请求帮助

(1) Will you do me a favor, please?

(2) Could you help us with our assignment?

(3) Leave him out of this, OK?

(4) Send me your picture, OK?

(5) Could you please pick up Mr. Davis at the airport?

11 Shopping
购 物

(1) Can I place an order for this CD?

(2) I'm looking for a tie to go with this shirt.

(3) What material is this made of?

(4) I'd like to exchange this for a larger size if it is possible.

(5) Sorry, we can't give you a discount.

(6) I take this, can I pay by credit card?

(7) Is there any special brand you'd like?

(8) We have various goods in different sizes.

(9) May I try it on?

(10) Please show me that one.

(11) I'm sorry, it is out of stock for the time being.

(12) It's to my taste.

(13) What style and color would you like?

(14) That's a bit more than I was expecting to pay.

(15) Could you cut the price a little, please?

(16) Let's go in and take a look.

12　Expression Your Opinion
阐明意见

(1) Let's get down to business.

(2) I'm not in a position to make a comment on it.

(3) If you insist on this point, then how about doing it in a different way?

(4) I'm afraid I disagree with you about this new project.

(5) We will let you know when we receive his reply to our offer.

(6) I'd recommend that you take an overall view of the situation.

(7) Your explanation doesn't make any sense to me.

(8) That's exactly what I've been thinking of.

(9) Sounds good to me. How about you?

(10) I'm not sure about how she will react.

(11) Please give us some time to think it over.

(12) We are not interested in this plan.

(13) I share your view on that.

(14) I couldn't have said it better.

(15) I don't think it will work.

(16) I get your point, but there are other things we have to consider.

(17) That's out of the question.

(18) I don't think anyone would disagree.

13 Complain
表达不满

(1) I hate to say this, but it's none of your business.

(2) You always make me do everything. Give me a break.

(3) I feel as if everything is going against me.

(4) What happened to us this morning was a disaster.

(5) He completed to me that task was too difficult to finish in a few days.

14 Appointments and Commitments
预约及承诺

(1) I'd like to make an appointment to meet your boss.

(2) Tell me what would be a good day for you.

(3) I'll let you know when and where to meet me.

(4) I'm off for the whole week.

(5) I'm afraid my schedule is too tight to make time to see you.

(6) Don't hesitate to change the time and place of our meeting.

(7) Let me know your convenience day.

(8) Hope to see you at your office on next Friday, namely December 25, 2019.

(9) I'd like to reserve a double room with an ocean view.

(10) Sure, you can pay by cash or by credit card.

15 The Complementary Close
正文结束语

(1) I'm looking forward to hearing from you.

(2) Hope to hear from you as soon as possible.

(3) We miss you a lot.

(4) We really miss you.

(5) Drop me a line when you have time.

(6) Thank you for your cooperation.

(7) Thank you for your time and trouble.

(8) Once again I want to thank you for your help.

(9) Please feel free to contact me if you have any question.

(10) Don't hesitate to contact me.

(11) Please reply as soon as possible.

(12) Your prompt reply would be very much appreciated.

(13) Thank you for your usual support.

(14) Waiting for your early reply.

(15) Let's keep in touch.

(16) Thank you again for your attention.

16 Greetings of Closing
结束问候语

(1) Best regards.

(2) Best wishes.

(3) Warmest regards.

(4) Warmest wishes.

(5) Please take care of yourself.

(6) God bless you.

(7) I wish you happiness and success in the future.

(8) Have a nice weekend.

(9) I hope you and your family have a good year.

(10) Hope you have an enjoyable stay here.

(11) Hope 2019 will be the best year for you and your family.

(12) Please give my best regards to your family.

(13) Please say hello to your family for me.

(14) Have a good journey.

(15) Very truly yours.

(16) Yours faithfully.

(17) Yours sincerely.

(18) Thanks and best regards.

Appendix 附 录

1 Common Abbreviations 函电常用缩写语

Ave.	——Avenue 街
ASAP	——As Soon as Possible 尽快
AUD	——Australian Dollar 澳元
Attn.	——Attention 收件人
ad.	——advertising 广告
ASN	——Advance Ship Notice 提前装船通知
Bldg.	——Building 建筑物
BCC.	——Blind Carbon Copy 密送
B/L	——Bill of lading 提单
B2B	——Business to Business 企业与企业的电子商务
B2C	——Business to Consumer 企业与消费者的电子商务
B/N	——Booking Note 托运单或订舱单
CAD	——Canadian Dollar 加币
CBD	——Central Business District 中央商务区
CEO	——Chief Executive Officer 首席执行官
Co.	——Company 公司
CC.	——Carbon Copy 抄送
C/D	——Customs Declaration 报关单
CIF	——Cost, Insurance and Freight 成本加保险费加运费
CFR	——Cost and Freight 成本加运费价

CY	——	Container Yard 集装箱堆场
CFS	——	Container Freight Station 集装箱货运站
CTN	——	Carton 纸箱
CQC	——	China Quality Certification Center 中国质量认证中心
DOZ	——	Dozen 一打,十二个
DOC	——	Document 文件,单据
DDP	——	Delivered Duty Paid 税后交货
EXW	——	EX WORKS 出厂价
EUR	——	Euro 欧元
EDI	——	Electronic Data Interchange 电子数据交换
ETA	——	Estimated Time of Arrival 估计到达时间
ETD	——	Estimated Time of Departure 预定出发时间
FOB	——	Free On Board 离岸价
FDA	——	Food and Drug Administration 美国食品药物管理局
GBP	——	Great Britain Pound 英镑
GDP	——	Gross Domestic Product 国民生产总值
G.W	——	Gross Weight 毛重
HKD	——	Hong Kong Dollar 港币
ICC	——	International Chamber of Commerce 国际商会
ISO	——	The International Organization for Standardization 国际标准化组织
Info.	——	Information 信息
Inc.	——	Incorporation 股份有限公司
IMP & EXP.	——	Import 进口 & Export 出口
IV	——	Invoice 发票
JPY	——	Japanese Yen 日元
JAS	——	Japanese Agriculture Standard 日本农林规格协会
JIT	——	Just in Time 准时化服务
Ltd.	——	Limited 股份有限公司
L/C	——	Letter of Credit 信用证
Mfg.	——	Manufacturing 制造
MAWB	——	Master Airway Bill 航空主运单
MBA	——	Master of Business Administration 工商管理硕士
N.W	——	Net Weight 净重
OEM	——	Original Equipment Manufacturing 贴牌生产
P.R.C	——	People's Republic of China 中华人民共和国

P.O.B. ——Post Office Box 邮政编码
PCS ——Pieces 件（复数）
P/L ——Packing List 装箱单
Ref. ——Reference 参考
RMB ——Ren Min Bi 人民币
USD ——Unite State of America Dollar 美元
VAT ——Value Added Tax 增值税
WTO ——World Trade Organization 世界贸易组织
WCO ——World Customs Organization 世界海关组织

2 Department and Job Title of Companies
公司常见部门及职务名称

部门名称		职务名称	
总公司	Head Office	董事长	chairman of the board
分公司	Branch Office	总经理	General Manager
运营部	Business Office	副总经理	Vice President
人事部	Personal Department	董事	Director
人力资源部	Human Resources Department	首席执行官	Chief Executive officer(CEO)
总务部	General Affairs Department	部门经理	Branch Manager
财务部	Accounting Department	财务总监	Chief Financial officer(CFO)
销售部	Sales Department	项目经理	Project Manager
市场部	Marketing Department	市场经理	Marketing Manager
运输部	Transportation Department	销售经理	Sales Manager
质量安全部	Quality and Safety Department	业务经理	Business Manager
修理部	Maintenance Department	技术总监	Chief Technical officer(CTO)
促销部	Sales Promotion Department	零售店经理	Retail Store Manager
国际部	International Department	销售助理	Sales Assistant
出口部	Export Department	销售主管	Sales Administrator
进口部	Import Department	外销部职员	Export Sales Stuff
公共关系部	Public Relations Department	销售代表	Marketing Representative
广告部	Advertising Department	生产线主管	Line Supervisor

续 表

部门名称		职务名称	
企划部	Planning Department	总代理	General Agency
产品开发部	Product development Department	独家代理	Sole Agency
研发部	Research and Development Department（P&D）	电脑操作员	Computer Operator
秘书室	Secretarial Pool	秘书	Secretary

3 World's Major Ports
世界主要港口

亚洲	译名/国家
Shanghai	上海（中国）
Qingdao	青岛（中国）
Dalian	大连（中国）
Guangzhou	广州（中国）
HongKong	香港（中国）
Gaoxiong	高雄（中国）
Kobe	神户港（日本）
Nagoya	名古屋（日本）
Osaka	大阪（日本）
Yokohama	横滨（日本）
Tokyo	东京（日本）
Pusan	釜山（韩国）
Bangkok	曼谷（泰国）
Beirut	贝鲁特（黎巴嫩）
Calcutta	加尔各答（印度）
Mumbai	孟买港（印度）
Chittagong	吉大港（孟加拉国）
Colombo	科伦坡（斯里兰卡）
Basra	巴士拉（伊拉克）
Jeddah	吉达（沙特阿拉伯）
Karachi	卡拉奇（巴基斯坦）
Manila	马尼拉（菲律宾）
Singapore	新加坡港（新加坡）

Rangoon	仰光（缅甸）
Danang	岘港（越南）
Haiphong	海防（越南）
Hanoi	河内（越南）
Jakarta	雅加达（印度尼西亚）
Tanjung Priok	丹绒布绿港（印度尼西亚）
Malacca	马六甲港（马来西亚）
Kuala Lumpur	吉隆坡（马来西亚）
Kuwait	科威特港（科威特）
Dubai	迪拜港（阿联酋）
Istanbul	伊斯坦布尔（土耳其）
Aden	亚丁（民主也门）

欧洲

London	伦敦（英国）
Southampton	南安普顿（英国）
Glasgow	格拉斯哥（英国）
Liverpool	利物浦（英国）
Bordeaux	波尔多（法国）
Marseilles	马赛（法国）
Bremen	不来梅（德国）
Bonn	波恩（德国）
Hamburg	汉堡（德国）
Rostock	罗斯托克（德国）
Bucharest	布加勒斯特（罗马尼亚）
Genoa	热那亚（意大利）
Naples	那不勒斯（意大利）
Venice	威尼斯（意大利）
Amsterdam	阿姆斯特丹（荷兰）
Rotterdam	鹿特丹（荷兰）
Bergen	卑尔根（挪威）
Oslo	奥斯陆（挪威）
Antwerp	安特卫普（比利时）
Barcelona	巴塞罗那（西班牙）
Gibraltar	直布罗陀（西班牙）
Setubal	塞图巴尔（葡萄牙）

Lisbon	里斯本(葡萄牙)
Gdansk	格但斯克(波兰)
Gdynia	格丁尼亚(波兰)
Leninggrad	列宁革勒(俄罗斯)
Saint Petersburg	圣彼得堡(俄罗斯)
Мурманск	摩尔曼斯克(俄罗斯)
Vladivostok	符拉迪沃斯托克/海参崴(俄罗斯)
Stockholm	斯德哥尔摩(瑞典)
Goteborg	哥德堡(瑞典)
Berne	伯尔尼(瑞士)
Copenhagen	哥本哈根(丹麦)
Reykjavik	雷克雅末克(冰岛)
Vaasa	瓦萨(芬兰)
Turku	土尔库(芬兰)
Helsinki	赫尔辛基(芬兰)
Poraeus	比雷埃夫斯(希腊)
Athens	雅典(希腊)

北美洲

Long Beach	长滩(美国)
Baltimore	巴尔的摩(美国)
Boston	波士顿(美国)
Honolulu	火奴鲁鲁(美国)
Houston	休斯敦(美国)
Los Angeles	洛杉矶(美国)
New Orleans	新奥尔良(美国)
New York	纽约(美国)
Philadelphia	费城(美国)
San Francisco	旧金山(美国)
Seattle	西雅图(美国)
Montreal	蒙特利尔(加拿大)
Quebec	魁北克(加拿大)
Vancouver	温哥华(加拿大)
Toronto	多伦多(加拿大)
Habana	哈瓦那(古巴)
Guaymas	瓜伊马斯(墨西哥)

南美洲

Buenos Aires	布宜诺斯艾利斯(阿根廷)
Bahia Blanca	布兰卡港(阿根廷)
Rio De Janeiro	里约热内卢(巴西)
Santos	圣多斯港(巴西)
Santiago	圣地亚哥(智利)
Valparaiso	瓦尔帕来索(智利)
Panama	巴拿马港(巴拿马)
Colón	科隆(巴拿马)
Caracas	加拉加斯(委内瑞拉)
Cartagena	卡塔赫纳(哥伦比亚)
Callao	卡亚俄(秘鲁)
Lima	利马(秘鲁)

非洲

Tunisia	突尼斯（突尼斯共和国）
Alexandria	亚历山大（埃及）
Cairo	开罗(埃及)
Tripoli	的黎波里(利比亚)
Luanda	罗达安港(安哥拉)
Doha	多哈(卡塔尔)
Durban	德班港(南非)
Capetown	开普敦港(南非)
Elizabeth	伊丽莎白港(南非)
Casablanca	卡萨布兰卡(摩洛哥)
Mombasa	蒙巴萨(肯尼亚)
Nairobi	内罗毕(肯尼亚)
Port Louis	路易港(毛里求斯)
Dakar	达喀尔(塞内加尔)
Dar Es Salaam	达累斯萨拉姆(坦桑尼亚)
Kinshasa	金沙萨(刚果)

大洋洲

Auckland	奥克兰(新西兰)
Wellington	惠林顿(新西兰)

Sydney	悉尼(澳大利亚)
Melbourne	墨尔本(澳大利亚)
Perth	珀斯(澳大利亚)
Port Moresby	莫尔兹比港(巴布亚新几内亚)
Suva	苏瓦(斐济)

References
参考文献

1. Ian Mackenzie. English for Business Studies [M]. London: Cambridge University, 2002.
2. 斯科特·奥伯.现代商务沟通[M].北京:中国人民大学出版社,2009.
3. Amanda Crandell Ju.商用英文情景口语100主题[M].许卉艳,译.北京:外文出版社,2009.
4. 滕美荣,许楠.外贸英语函电[M].北京:首都经济贸易大学出版社,2011.
5. 郑淑媛.外贸英语函电[M].北京:北京出版社,2014.
6. 舒红.国际贸易的潜规则[J].品牌,2015.
7. 邢理平.商务与环境英语阅读[M].北京:中国传媒大学出版社,2015.
8. 黄俐波.国际贸易实务[M].杭州:浙江大学出版社,2015.
9. 刘练.新编外贸英语函电实务[M].长沙:湖南师范大学出版社,2016.
10. 孟令超.实战剑桥国际商务英语[M].北京:中国传媒大学出版社,2016.